Get Out of the Boat

A JOURNEY TO WHAT YOUR SOUL
LONGS FOR

Susan Alford Ashcraft, PhD

TRILOGY CHRISTIAN PUBLISHERS
Tustin, CA

Trilogy Christian Publishers
A Wholly Owned Subsidiary of Trinity Broadcasting Network
2442 Michelle Drive
Tustin, CA 92780

Get Out of the Boat: A Journey to What Your Soul Longs For

For information, address Trilogy Christian Publishing

Rights Department, 2442 Michelle Drive, Tustin, CA 92780.

Trilogy Christian Publishing/ TBN and colophon are trademarks of Trinity Broadcasting Network.

For information about special discounts for bulk purchases, please contact Trilogy Christian Publishing.

Manufactured in the United States of America

Trilogy Disclaimer: The views and content expressed in this book are those of the author and may not necessarily reflect the views and doctrine of Trilogy Christian Publishing or the Trinity Broadcasting Network.

10 9 8 7 6 5 4 3 2 1

Library of Congress Cataloging-in-Publication Data is available.

ISBN: 978-1-68556-923-5

E-ISBN: 978-1-68556-924-2)

Contents

Dedication

For Kaity and Cara, remarkable women, who are altogether lovely, and none compare.

And for Del, God knew.

It Won't Be Easy, But It Will Be Simple

The journey to what your soul longs for...

Nine little words, nothing fancy or extraordinary about them when we consider them individually. But, when they are strung together to make a phrase, these simple words become quite significant. These words create meaning, illustrate purpose, and communicate emotion. They represent a place, a time, and a destination.

Words have always been important to me. They wield incredible power in our lives, whether we recognize it or not. Words reveal the truth. They can also create lies. Words can invoke happiness, laughter, and acceptance. And yet, they can also lead us to experience great sorrow and pain. Words can bring us peace, but they can also readily destroy us in mind and spirit. Words bring people together and tear them apart. Words are potent and formidable in their ability to shape us—our thoughts, emotions, and actions.

The word I consider to be the most compelling word in scripture is beloved. Found multiple times in both the Old and New Testaments, beloved comes from two root words in Hebrew, meaning to breathe and to long for. In the original Greek, the word used for beloved means to prefer. It is the word used, repeatedly, to declare God's infinite love for His beloved Son, Jesus Christ. Numerous passages of scripture cite the word beloved as a representation of God's love for His people. It is beautiful, awe-inspiring, and sacred. The term beloved signifies God's love for His chosen—His daughters—you and me.

I am my beloved's, and my beloved is mine.
Song of Songs 6:3

When God calls us His beloved, it literally means that He longs for us—we are His breath—He prefers us—we are His. He loves us unconditionally beyond our comprehension. God loves us completely and without reservation. He loves us simply for who we are, not for who we can or will be. He loves us as He loves His Son. We are His beloved.

It's difficult to wrap your mind around this reality. This message of God's love for us can be difficult to hear amid the noise around us, and even harder to accept. I know it was for me. Because the world we live in today is almost void of this pure expression of love, we believe we can only be loved for what do or how we look, or how we make another person feel. We believe we must earn love. Nothing could be farther from the truth! This type of love is based on contingency. It is a selfish love built on giving and taking—a love that feels more like a commodity than a gift. You must do something, give something, or be something, to trade for someone's love, affirmation, or even acceptance. Worldly love, however, is not the love God, our Father, our Creator, has for us. Thank goodness!

God's love is categorically and completely given to us because we are His unique creation. We don't have to earn it. We already have it! From the moment we are created until we breathe our last breath and even beyond, we are beloved by Him. He sees us. He values us. He cares for us. He loves and adores us. And our souls long to believe these truths. My soul—your soul—longs to be loved.

The moment I had this beautiful realization was the moment I began my own journey to finding what my soul had always longed for. It wasn't easy. Change never is. Growth can sometimes be painful and awkward. Moving from one place or state of mind to another requires effort and desire. And yet, it is worth every step.

They say teachers are the worst students! They, whoever they are, may be right. It sure did take me a while to learn and I had the best teacher of all: God my Father, my Creator, my Beloved. He is the ultimate professor in the classroom of life. Fortunately, our professor gave us a textbook for this life course: The Holy Bible, His Word, our guidebook to becoming His beloved in every way. His words are true. His words are steady, secure, and eternal just like his love for us.

Will you join me in this adventure into the unknown to finally discover the known?

Beloved, the journey to what your soul longs for won't be easy, but it will be simple. Let's go.

Get Out of the Boat

I went out west on a road trip with my husband. We flew out to Washington state, rented a car, and drove 2,800 miles through seven states visiting the great national parks of our country. It was amazing. I've never seen a country so big and wide, especially Montana. If you have ever driven out that way, you know the towns are far apart and you can go miles without passing another car. We talked and listened to 80's music and audiobooks to pass the time.

Now as a kid, traveling with my parents, before iPads, smartphones, Spotify, and little screens in minivans playing movies, we would have to get creative to pass the time on long road trips. My family liked to sing, loudly and with lots of feeling to be sure. Anyway, as the firstborn, I liked to lead and then my sisters would join in, and we would have a round. My favorite was a song about a little boat. You probably know it, *Row, row, row your boat gently down the stream. Merrily, merrily, merrily, merrily, life is but a dream.* Rowing a boat down a stream? Merrily? Sounds like a lot of work to me!

I want us to spend a few minutes talking about boats. I think there is much we can learn from them. And I want to start with a wonderful story found in the Book of Matthew. It's about a certain boat. The vessel was filled with a group of twelve men, who were rowing as hard and as fast as they could. But a powerful storm was making their journey far from merry or dreamy for that matter.

Now Jesus had just fed the 5,000 by multiplying the loaves and fishes—a really cool miracle. It was a time of great celebration, but now after they had eaten and cleaned up, Jesus told His disciples to get into the boat and go across the Sea of Galilee to Capernaum. He told them He would meet them later on the other side.

> *Immediately after this, Jesus insisted that his disciples get back into the boat and cross to the other side of the lake, while he sent the people home. After sending them home, he went up into the hills by himself to pray. Night fell while he was there alone. Meanwhile, the disciples were in trouble far away from land, for a strong wind had risen, and they were fighting heavy waves. About three o'clock in the morning, Jesus came toward them, walking*

on the water. When the disciples saw him walking on the water, they were terrified. In their fear, they cried out, "It's a ghost!" But Jesus spoke to them at once. "Don't be afraid," he said. "Take courage. I am here!"

Matthew 14: 22-27 (NLT)

Let's look more closely at this passage. The boat the disciples are in is a long way from land. It's 6-7 miles across the Sea of Galilee and it's 3 a.m.! They had started their journey right after dinner. Basically, these fishermen have been furiously rowing their boat for about 8-9 hours and they have only made it about ½ way across a 7-mile expanse of water. This was no merry stream!

Why? Because a storm has "beaten," battered," and "thrashed" their boat. They must have been exhausted and ready to give up. And to make matters worse, the disciples think they see a ghost.

Have you ever been afraid? I mean really afraid. I mean you can't breathe, you want to run, but your legs won't move and besides that, there's nowhere to go. It's that "I Know What You Did Last Summer afraid!" That's exactly what the disciples felt. All night they have been pummeled by the wind and water. And now they are seeing ghosts? They must have been asking themselves if they were going crazy? If they would make it? Would they sink? Would they die?

Then they realize: it's not a ghost at all. It's Jesus, their rabbi, striding across the water.

> *Then Peter called to him, "Lord, if it's really you, tell me to come to you, walking on the water." "Yes, come," Jesus said. So Peter went over the side of the boat and walked on the water toward Jesus. But when he saw the strong wind and the waves, he was terrified and began to sink. "Save me, Lord!" he shouted. Jesus immediately reached out and grabbed him. "You have so little faith," Jesus said. "Why did you doubt me?" When they (Peter and Jesus) climbed back into the boat, the wind stopped. Then the disciples worshiped him. "You really are the Son of God!" they exclaimed.*
>
> Matthew 14:28-32

Peter is exhausted, weary, and weak. He has been rowing for hours. He is afraid. There is a storm, and no matter how hard he tries, he can't manage or conquer it. And he is a fisherman by trade! My goodness, sailing is what he does for a living. But, throughout the long hard night, Peter has failed to change his situation. When Peter recognizes Jesus, all he wants to do is be with Him. He's not sure how he will get to Jesus. He just knows he must get there.

You've got to admire Peter's courage. I would have been scared to death to get out of that boat into the thrashing waves. There is a well-known and popular saying that explains Peter's action quite well. "Courage is not the absence of fear, it is the presence of fear, yet the will to continue!"

I think Peter's desire to join Jesus on the water was an expression of his need to rise above the storm, his circumstance. He wanted to go beyond the range or limit of the situation he found himself in at that moment. Peter wanted out of where he was. The boat wasn't safe anymore, the storm was raging, and he didn't want to die. But more than that, Peter wanted to be with Jesus. Jesus was his safe place, his protector, and his provider. His need for Jesus trumped his fear about his present circumstance.

You see, Peter is willing to risk and trust to be with Jesus. Peter steps into the actual churning water and blowing winds to get to Jesus. Are you kidding? Remember, the storm is still raging. Here is our first compelling lesson: Peter must get out of the boat (what he knows) and walk through the storm (what he doesn't know) to get to Jesus. When Jesus allows Peter to walk on the water toward Him, Jesus is changing not only Peter's perspective but his trajectory in life.

Some time ago, I was faced with the same choice Peter had. I was in the middle of the biggest, worst storm I have ever experienced in my life. One night, in the fourth watch, I had to decide if I was going to continue rowing my boat or get out into the churning water and risk to trust.

After graduating from college, I had big plans. I was going to marry a man I loved, and he would love me. We would be faithful to each other and God. We would raise a beautiful family together. My plan, also my dream, was to return to my alma mater. But this time, I wouldn't be the student. I would be the teacher. Of course, this would require a lot more education, experience, and hard work, but I was motivated to achieve. So, I rowed my proverbial boat (my life), across the sea, as hard and as fast as I could, in that very direction.

Over the course of the next several years, I achieved all my plans and dreams, but one. I became a psychology professor at a university. I got married. I gave birth to two remarkable and beautiful daughters. I was faithful to God and to my husband. But my husband was not faithful to me. He didn't honor the covenant, our promise, that we had made to one another on our wedding day.

For twenty-four years, I rowed my boat through a storm I never imagined I would find myself in. My dreams of a perfect little life were sucked into a black hole and disappeared into oblivion. My husband's multiple infidelities, deceit, verbal and emotional abuse kept my girls and me in a perpetual state of anxiety and pain. The storm I was rowing in was continuous. Over the years, it only grew in intensity. It was like a hurricane really. One that starts as a Category 1 storm and as it gets closer to land it builds into a devastating Category 5. You know, the most destructive storm there is and the one that causes the most casualties.

My marriage was a hurricane, and at first, I was the only casualty, but as the years progressed, and my girls were born, the storm built in intensity. The girls became casualties too. Unfortunately, I discovered too late that the longer you continue in an unhealthy relationship, the more accustomed you get to it—its patterns, experiences, and outcomes. You get comfortable in your pain. The suffering and anxiety are what you expect, it's what you know, it's what you think you deserve.

As a result, my boat was battered and damaged inside by anxiety and rejection. I believed I had no worth. I beat myself up for being a failure as a wife. I told myself that if I just worked harder; if I just changed myself enough; if I just kept it all together; if I just forgave him one more time; my boat would conquer the storm and sail into peaceful waters. If I, if I, if I—sound familiar?

I was a broken record, a boat with so many holes, I couldn't patch them fast enough. Now, for anyone on the outside looking in, my boat looked great, it was pretty, shiny, and a place of happiness and success. No one suspected that the inside was dark, in shambles, and a deep hole of desperation. I rowed my boat, refusing to give up, and at the expense of my well-being and my girls. I naively attempted to make everything appear like it was working even though it was failing miserably. But I am loyal and perseverant. I decided I would find a way to row my boat through this storm.

Ironic that every day, I walked into my classroom and taught my students strategies for healthy relationships. I encouraged them to be committed to the pursuit of a relationship with God, their spouse, and their future children. Then, I came home and faced the reality of my own unhealthy, abusive, and deteriorating marriage.

I understand now why I held on for so long. I believed in marriage. I believed in family. These were holy and sacred relationships to me. Meant to last. Meant to persevere. Meant to be relationships of safety, security, growth, and love. Not only did I believe these truths I had decided to dedicate my professional career to the study and celebration of the covenant of marriage, the gifts of family, and sexuality. There was no way I could give up. I didn't want to admit that my marriage was a failure.

Fast forward through twenty-four years of marriage and nothing had changed, it had only gotten worse. It did not matter how hard I tried to make things right. After discovering yet another indiscretion by my husband, my faith and trust were shattered completely. I finally accepted the reality of my situation. He was not willing to change—to make this marriage and family work. So, I found myself right where Peter was so many years ago. The storm was raging, I was exhausted. I had reached the end of my efforts. I knew I couldn't row any longer.

Make no mistake, I did not at this time in my life have big faith—my faith was hanging by a thread. But, with my faith as small as a mustard seed, I made one of the most significant decisions in my life. I climbed out of my boat into the churning water. I desired to be with Jesus above all else. I needed Him to save me from drowning.

But, like Peter, I saw the wind and I lost focus. I allowed the circumstances around me to fill me with doubt. You see, as soon as I climbed out of the boat and filed for divorce, I was hit by a gust of wind so strong it knocked me over. For so long, I had been totally focused on rowing through a relational storm. I did not even suspect or know there was another even more damaging storm raging around me. I discovered not only was my marriage a lie but so was almost everything in my life. I realized I had never known my husband and that I had no clue about what and who he really was. Long story short, he went to prison and is now a convicted felon. And although he took much from others, he took everything from his family.

There I was, placing my trust in Jesus, walking toward Him, and I quickly found myself homeless, bankrupt, and with no car. I couldn't get to my job, and I couldn't get my girls to school. I had no insurance and no credit. I had been so focused on keeping my marriage together, changing myself to please him. I was doing all I could so that the people in my world wouldn't see the dysfunction in my life and family, that I had missed the reality and depth of my husband's deceit.

I sunk into the cold, dark water. I snapped. I started screaming on the inside and on the outside. Why Lord? I thought I could trust you. I went all in God, I believed you would take care of me! Where are you?

It was the lowest point in my life. I didn't know how I would make it. Right then and there I decided that the Lord's promises and dreams that I had built my life on may have been true for people in the Bible. Even for other people in my life but there was no way they were true for me. Then I wept. Help me, Lord—save me—just like Peter.

The very next day, after raging at God most of the night, I came to school (my dad gave me a ride). I was sitting at my desk grading papers, trying not to weep. Someone knocked on my door. Someone I knew well, an angel sent in my time of need. This person came in and laid a set of keys on my desk and said, "I have an old car I need to get rid of because I'm getting a new one. I was praying last night, and the Lord put you in my mind. I don't know why, but I feel impressed to give the car to you. It's not worth much but it will get you wherever you need to go."

> *What's more, I am with you, and I will protect you wherever you go. One day I will bring you back to this land. I will not leave you until I have finished giving you everything I have promised you.*
>
> Genesis 28:15

I could hear Jesus saying to me at that moment, "Oh Susan, you of little faith? Why did you doubt me?"

Today, I am a witness, to His love, care, provision, protection, and grace. That car, which my girls and I affectionately dubbed our "Jesus car," was just the first of more miracles than I have space to share. I am a living example of a life restored. Jesus carried me through that storm. He climbed into my boat and brought peace to my life and to my girls. He surrounded me with my university family who loved and encouraged me through it all. He positioned family and friends around me for support. He brought a godly man into my life who loves me and my girls. My gift from God is a husband and father who puts God first and is a servant leader in our home.

Now, it is my turn to give back. It is time for what was meant for evil in my life to be used for good in yours. As I sit here writing this, I imagine all of you who might one day read my story. When I consider you in my mind's eye, I see hundreds of boats on a vast expanse of water. Boats of all shapes and sizes. Boats that have been battered or maybe wrecked. Boats that look great on the outside but are falling apart on the inside. Like mine was. Boats that are being captained by your expectations, your goals, your stubbornness, your selfishness, and your refusal to accept the truth. Boats that are not captained by Jesus, the only one who can steer you in the right direction.

Maybe you are rowing the "I Don't Matter" boat?

You believe you don't have value. You believe you have no worth because that's what the people in your life have told you or shown you by their actions. You've been rejected, bullied, or maybe you just don't know how to find your place in this big world. And if you believe you don't matter to others, how could you matter to God?

Or the "I've Done Too Much" boat?

You've made some choices you aren't proud of. You've made mistakes that you believe are unforgivable. Maybe you are struggling with an addiction. Maybe it's pornography, maybe it's alcohol, drugs, or food. Or maybe it is a relationship, one in which you compromised yourself to feel loved or valued. And you sit in your boat wrestling with your constant companions: shame and guilt. You tell yourself there are no do-overs in life—I'm dirty now--so why would God want a relationship with me? Why would anyone want a relationship with me?

Are you rowing the "I'm Damaged" boat?

You've been abused, manipulated, taken advantage of, and lied to. You've experienced so much pain in your life at the hands of others that you are afraid to trust. Maybe someone you loved has hurt you so deeply and broken your trust so completely that you don't believe you can ever trust again, especially God. You are angry, anxious, broken, and maybe even hopeless.

Maybe you are hanging out in the "I Don't Know What to Do" boat?

You are being tossed around, with no clear direction in your life. You are afraid to step out and risk a relationship with Him. You are not sure what your purpose is or where you are going. You are for the first time on your own and in a storm of uncertainty and fear.

Bottom line, whatever boat you are rowing, whatever storm you are in, we all wonder and ask ourselves the same questions. How can I trust God? His promises? His love for me? Sure, maybe that works for others, but for me? No way! You are afraid to get out of your boat and walk on the water because no matter how ugly, lonely, dark, empty, or turbulent your boat is—it's yours and it's comfortable.

Perhaps, the most common mistake we can make when we read this Bible story is thinking it's solely about Peter. People will say, "Look at Peter's faith, or lack of faith and look at what we can learn from Peter." The reality in this story, like all other stories in the Bible, it's about Jesus. This is a story about a Savior that didn't take his eyes off Peter, even when Peter took his eyes off Him. Peter lost hope in Jesus's ability to save, but Jesus remained faithful even when Peter wasn't. When Peter took his eyes off Jesus, Jesus never took his eyes off him.

As someone who rowed their boat for far too many hours, who gave up hope that she was worth saving, who didn't believe there was any way out, who in the fourth watch of the night risked it all to walk toward Jesus, I am standing here today to say—you can trust Jesus. He knows what he is doing, His promises are true, and He will never take His eyes off you. From beginning to end.

> *And be sure of this: I am with you always, even to the end of the age.*
>
> Matthew 28:20

Be encouraged to recognize and embrace this reality: there is no storm too wild, too devastating, too incredibly big that Jesus cannot bring you out of into a place of calm and easy waters. But it will require something of you—TRUST. I believe trusting is one of the most difficult things a person will ever do. Trust requires a combination of feeling, thought, and action. There is no better place to begin this exercise than here right now at this moment in time. It won't be easy to get out of your boat. But, when you do walk to Him, the rest of the journey becomes simple.

Let's not forget how the story ended.

> *When they (Peter and Jesus) climbed back into the boat, the wind stopped.*
>
> Matthew 14:32

When Peter decided that to be with Jesus in the stormy sea was better than being in his familiar boat something incredible happened. The scripture is clear. The storm didn't stop. In fact, Jesus and Peter walked across the water through the storm back to the boat. And when Peter and Jesus got in the boat—the wind ceased, and the storm stopped. Peter's trust—his desire for his Savior—got him out of his boat. Walking toward Jesus—sinking because he lost focus in the storm—crying out for help—is a picture of how Peter struggled to maintain trust and live it out. It is a picture that should be titled, "We can't make it through this life without Him no matter how hard we might try."

Our trust in Him invites Him to walk with us through the storm and into our lives where He can restore and make new—where the storm ceases and peace is found.

It's time to get out of your boat, beloved.

Look in the Mirror

Mirror, mirror on the wall, who is the fairest of them all?

The first animated movie I remember seeing as a child was *Snow White*. And it made a huge impression on me. A beautiful princess who was kind, gentle and perfect. Everyone loved her, the animals, the dwarves, and Prince Charming. Everyone, except for the wicked queen. She was jealous of Snow White. The queen wanted what she didn't have. When she looked into the mirror, she didn't see her own reflection only a distorted image that fueled the fire of her envy. So, she was willing to do awful things to herself (drink a potion and turn herself into an old crone) just to beat out the competition.

I'm ashamed to admit it but I have had periods in my life where I was much more like that queen than Snow White. You see, throughout my adolescent and adult life, I have struggled at times with my reflection when I gazed into the mirror. But it wasn't always this way.

When I was in elementary school, I lived with my family, in a house that could only be described as "groovy" by today's standards. Wall-to-wall gold shag carpeting, dark wood-paneled walls, avocado green bathroom fixtures, and a sunken living room. My favorite feature of my childhood home was the mirrored tile wall in the main hall. Spanning the total height and width of the wall in our ranch-style house, you had to pass it on your way to any room. I used to look at myself in that full wall-sized mirror and make funny faces. I would practice my dance moves and check out all my outfits when my sister and I were playing dress-up. Often, I would just sit and look intently at the image that was reflected there.

We moved from that house to another and regrettably the mirrored wall didn't make it on the truck. But there were plenty of mirrors in our new house, in fact, in most rooms. It wasn't long before, I started using the mirrors in my bathroom and bedroom to check my appearance before going to school or to measure myself against the current beauty standard of the day. I began to focus more on what I considered to be my flaws and imperfections instead of the happy self-assured curious child that I had left behind at my groovy house with the mirrored wall.

Fast forward to adulthood, my mirror time continued to destroy my confidence one little piece at a time.

I can be hard on myself. Without fail, when I do, I am quick to pass judgment on myself. It's funny that I wouldn't put up with other people being harsh critics, but I will be my own worst critic. And the more criticism I speak over myself, the cloudier my reflection becomes in the mirror. And I know that I am not alone.

What does the research say?

- 63% of female participants identified weight as the key factor in determining how they felt about themselves – more important than family, school, or career.
- 86% of all women are dissatisfied with their bodies and want to lose weight.
- For women, being at the beach in their bathing suits (38%), shopping for clothes (44%), and trying on old clothes they haven't worn in a while (35%) are especially likely to trigger negative thoughts about their body image.
- 8 out of 10 women will not attend important events if they don't like how they look.
- By age 13, 53% of American girls are unhappy with their bodies. By age 17, this percentage has increased to 78%.
- By age 6, girls start to express concerns about their own weight or shape.

- 40-60% of elementary school girls (ages 6-12) are concerned about their weight or about becoming too fat.

  (Statistics reported in research by the following: The National Institute of Health, John Hopkins University, Loma Linda University, National Eating Disorders Association, The National Institute on Media and Family, and Ipsos.)

It's all about body image. We all have one and it's deeply personal. Body image can be defined as the way in which we view our physical self, and the thoughts and feelings we experience because of our view. A woman's body image is molded throughout her life by her interactions with a variety of sources: family, peers, media, culture, school, church, and many other experiences. It is also shaped by her beliefs about beauty, value, and worth.

Psychologists suggest that there are four aspects of body image that when combined create a positive or negative evaluation: perceptual, affective, cognitive, and behavioral.

What do you see when you look at your body?

Perceptual Body Image is the way you see your body. Your perception of your body doesn't always match the reality of your physical appearance. You might see yourself as overweight when you are not.

How do you feel about your body?

Affective Body Image is the emotional experience of body image. Your level of satisfaction, high to low, regarding your weight, shape, or individual physical features will influence your feelings. You might feel uncomfortable with the shape of your body.

What do you think about your body?

Cognitive Body Image includes both our negative and positive thoughts about our body. These thinking patterns can lead to acceptance or preoccupation and obsession. You might think about your weight daily.

What do you do because of how you see, feel, and think about your body?

Behavioral Body Image is the way in which our body image impacts our actions or behaviors. These behaviors can be healthy or unhealthy. You might starve yourself or isolate yourself from others because of your unhappiness with your body.

Because body image is the result of our seeing, feeling, thinking, and doing, we actually do have quite a bit of control over it. When a woman accepts, appreciates, and respects her body, she possesses a positive body image. When a woman rejects, diminishes, and punishes her body, she is living with a negative body image.

The most used object to view and evaluate our body image is a mirror. We look in mirrors every day, often multiple times. And because we are living in a society that equates one's physical beauty and outward appearance with one's intrinsic value, we judge ourselves harshly. And we are experiencing the consequences of this perspective. An emphasis on physical attractiveness as the definition of self is detrimental to our emotional health and well-being and even our physical health. Nowhere is this emphasis on physical perfection found to a greater degree than in all forms of modern media.

We are bombarded constantly by images of what we should look like and what we fail to look like. Television, movies, advertisements, the internet, and streaming platforms, all show us an image of perfection that we should all strive for. And if we don't meet it, then we should try harder. Social media, with billions of users every day, is the worst offender.

Social media images are designed to present the best version of a person. We don't want the world to see us as we really are. We want them to see what we imagine ourselves to be. We filter and photoshop ourselves – virtually and in reality – for so much of our lives that we often forget what's underneath. Or, perhaps, we try to forget. Our social media posts are just billboards— highlights of our lives. We are judging ourselves and our lives based on billboards advertising fabricated ideals.

If we are constantly exposed to the ideal image, our evaluation of ourselves is based on unrealistic standards. This exposure and comparison distort our view of who we are. Whether it's Instagram, Tik Tok, Facebook, Snapchat, or all the above, the use of any of these platforms has been linked to the development of a negative body image.

What does the research say?

- In 2020, over 3.6 billion people were using social media worldwide and this number is projected to increase to almost 4.41 billion in 2025.
- Women are less likely to be happy with their bodies if they spend more than an hour a day on social media.
- Children and teenagers spend somewhere between 6-9 hours per day using some form of media.
- 88% of women who use social media compare themselves to the images they see there.
- Instagram and TikTok images which typically feature beautiful people doing exercise, or at least pretending, create harsh self-judgments.
- Spending a lot of time perfecting a "selfie" is a potential sign that someone is struggling with body dissatisfaction.

(Statistics reported in research published by the following: The National Institute of Health, National Eating Disorders Association, Common Sense Media, Illinois State University, University of London, King University and Statista Research Department)

Social media use changes the way you perceive your own body! The effects of the media on a girl's or woman's development have been well-documented—depression, anxiety, jealousy, loneliness, eating disorders, early sexualization, low self-esteem, and even self-harm among females of all ages. Our obsession with outer beauty and physical perfection leads many of us to ride a rollercoaster of binging, purging, extreme exercising, and starvation in pursuit of the unattainable. It's toxic!

How harshly do you judge yourself? Your facial features? Your body? Your hair? Your skin? Your weight?

I remember the day I had the most painful reality check of my life. I was having a bad day, you know the kind where you feel bloated, tired, and nothing you put on passes muster. One of those days where you say to yourself, "Ugh, I hate my body, it doesn't matter what I wear, I'm still gonna look awful!"

I was standing in front of my full-length mirror in my bathroom, multiple outfits crumpled on the floor after trying them on in disgust, becoming more anxious and negative by the second. Only this day, I wasn't running these negative and demeaning comments over and over in my mind, instead, I was saying them out loud at an increasing volume. And the more I talked to my reflection, the worse the words became.

Hot tears filled my eyes and I beat my hand on the mirror and said, "So ugly! God, why did you make me this way?"

I was startled when I heard my eight-year-old daughter's small voice, "Mommy, does that mean I'm ugly too? Cause I look like you."

I have never felt so ashamed of myself as I did at that moment.

For the first time in a very long time, I looked, really looked, at my face in the mirror. I was grieved to see how unhappy and anxious I looked. My eyes were hollow looking back at me. I was a shadow of my former self. I had become a woman I didn't recognize. In my relentless pursuit of a perfected self, I'd lost touch with my true self. I had spent the better part of my young adult life measuring myself against an ideal that was not of God but of the world. I am made in the image of God, and I am beloved by Him—I am a woman of highest worth. Nothing else matters.

This was my initial step in a journey back to the happy, self-assured, curious child that would make funny faces in the mirrored wall. I decided to look in the mirror and instead of criticizing; I would try to praise instead. I studied my reflection and noted all the physical features that God had given me. Then, I thanked him for each one—my red hair, my pale skin, my freckles, my shape, my height—each physical feature that was me.

I tried to imagine how God saw me. I know how I see each one of my daughters—beautiful, vibrant, sparkling with joy, there is no one like them. That's how God sees me because I am his daughter—his beloved creation. My uniqueness, my quirks, my beauty, my laughter, my sorrow, and my suffering, all of me is beautiful because it is the full representation of me. Not just the parts I want others to see, not just the parts I want to hide—it's all of me.

This mirror exercise helped me gain a different perspective—one of love and compassion for myself. Instead of relying on other people for affirmation and validation, I turned instead to the One who loves me most and best. God's love is not based on my ability to be perfect in face and form! Here is the truth, beloved. You are visible, significant, useful, desired, beautiful, loved, and never forgotten. He longs for us to have an appropriate sense of self-worth—one rooted in Him and His love.

Some years ago, I looked in the mirror, and staring at my reflection, I asked my Creator a single question, "Am I beautiful?"

My soul jumped when he answered. *"You are Mine created by My hand. Dwell in My Word, beloved, your answer is there."*

I went to His word. I was filled with an overwhelming need to read, to study and understand, to pour over my Father's words that were written to me, about me, and for me. Here is what I discovered in my search.

You are altogether beautiful, my darling, beautiful in every way.

Song of Songs 4:7

You made all the delicate, inner parts of my body and knit me together in my mother's womb. Thank you for making me so wonderfully complex! Your workmanship is marvelous—how well I know it.

Psalms 139:13-14

Because you are precious to me. You are honored, and I love you.

Isaiah 43:4

For we are God's masterpiece. He has created us anew in Christ Jesus, so we can do the good things he planned for us long ago.

Ephesians 2:10

And yet, O Lord, you are our Father. We are the clay, and you are the potter. We all are formed by your hand.

Isaiah 64:8

The Lord doesn't see things the way you see them. People judge by outward appearance, but the Lord looks at the heart.

I Samuel 16:7

The Lord will hold you in his hand for all to see a
splendid crown in the hand of God. Isaiah 62:3
So don't be afraid; you are more valuable to God
than a whole flock of sparrows.

Matthew 10:31

I am beautiful, but that's not all I am. I am valuable and worthy. I am created by Him and for Him. I am a masterpiece—His masterpiece.

I want to challenge you to start using a different measuring stick when you look in the mirror—God's word. Consider, maybe for the first time in a long time or maybe even for the very first time, not measuring your worth by attaining the "perfect body," "perfect face," or "perfect life." Trade those thoughts in for God's truth. He is the creator of beauty, and He is the only one who can define it.

Imagine how different each of our lives would look if we took God's Word to heart and embraced the Bible's teachings on beauty. What if we truly recognized that they were written for us? I believe when we do our reflection softens and becomes radiant. When we know who we are in our Father's eyes and we turn our faces unashamedly towards Him, we truly embrace what it means to be His daughter. We are beautiful because He is!

Look in the mirror, beloved, and love the woman you see smiling back at you.

Unpack Your Suitcase

When I was fourteen, I was in California at a church revival with my parents. My dad was leading music that week and we had been at every service. I will always remember the last night because it was life-changing for me. The atmosphere was electric. It is still vivid in my mind because it was my first personal encounter with the Holy Spirit. It was the night I seriously vowed to put God first in my life and pursue, really pursue, a relationship with Him.

But then the revival was over, we left California and drove cross-country back home to Tennessee. We visited the Grand Canyon, a Navajo reservation, and swam in a pool shaped like a flamingo. Needless to say, the life-changing service and my vow to really pursue God became a distant memory. Life moved on.

As I grew into adulthood, other things became a priority—school, relationships, myself, my career, and my children. I spent more time pursuing these other things in my life than I did on my knees and in the Word. I still believed. I still prayed. I still pursued a Christ-like life, I just didn't make Him number one in all things. And that's when my life began to unravel. I hadn't forgotten the vow I made when I was fourteen, but I sure did forget its significance in every facet of my life.

Let me clue you in on some important truths I have learned since that service so long ago in California. Walking with God, putting Him first, following His Word, and doing the best that I could do with myself, my family, and everyone else in my life, didn't get me a free pass to avoid challenges, temptations, or loneliness. Neither the moment I called Jesus, my Savior, the night my adolescent self-made a vow to God, nor the day I was baptized into the church were the moments in which my life got perfect or easy. In fact, looking back, my life was anything but the blissful dream I thought it would be when I became a Christian. Sure, there were some incredibly satisfying moments, miracles, and happiness. But there were also times of great challenge, heartbreak, devastation, and failure.

There were days in my life—years even when I questioned if God had abandoned me. I felt so alone. I didn't feel like He heard me or even cared that I was hurting. Of course, this wasn't true, but I was so focused on my mistakes and hurt from the past—the loneliness and hopelessness of my present—and the worry and dread I felt even contemplating my future, that I wouldn't have heard or felt God, even if He knocked me over the head! In fact, there were times, the weight of it all—everything I was carrying—was just too much. I was overwhelmed. I believed my poor choices, my failures, and my imperfections were burdens I would carry for the rest of my life.

The truth is God loves me no matter what—period. His son, Jesus Christ, died to save me but not because He didn't love me already. He loves me despite me. My belief that God had forgotten me was a circumstance of my own making. God will never leave me or forsake me. I just couldn't see past my own pain to embrace this truth. I needed to give my burden to Him. I didn't need to carry it any longer. But I struggled to let Him have it. My actions were putting a wall between me and God.

> *So be strong and courageous! Do not be afraid and do not panic. For the Lord your God will personally go ahead of you. He will neither fail you nor abandon you.*
>
> Deuteronomy 31:6

"I will never leave you or abandon you." This phrase is found in multiple places throughout scripture, in both the Old and New Testaments. It's God's promise to us, one He makes repeatedly. No matter our past or present, God will never not be at our side. He loves us unconditionally. Why is this truth so difficult for us to believe? Okay, I'm going to just say it. It is an awful word—one no one likes to hear much less talk about unless it belongs to someone else.

Shame

It is the painful and self-conscious feeling of humiliation or distress you experience because of a negative and critical evaluation of the self. Shame reflects how you feel about yourself. It's that horrible feeling in the pit of your stomach that twists painfully. It makes you want to hide and never show your face again. Shame squeezes you in a vice so tight, that you can't breathe. Shame so clouds our vision that we cannot see the truth of God's love for us.

In developmental psychology, we study emotions that are associated with the human experience. At our birth, we all have the capacity as infants to express joy, sadness, anger, fear, and disgust. God wired all of us with five basic emotions. Think about Pixar's Inside Out! Notice what's not on this list? Shame. And yet, shame is a universal experience—people—men and women—of all ages—from all cultures, environments, and regions experience shame.

Shame is an emotion we learn from the people in our world after we are born. It can be taught, modeled, spoken over us and into us. It is a favorite weapon of bullies and those who feel so inadequate they must hurt others to feel good about themselves. I believe shame gives you an inaccurate view of yourself. If left unchecked, shame can become chronic and make you believe that you are in some way fundamentally flawed. It can have catastrophic effects on our psyche.

Don't confuse shame with guilt. They are not the same emotions or responses. Guilt is the feeling of worry or unhappiness that you experience if you have done something wrong. You feel guilty about what you did. Guilt focuses on the action. Guilt says I did something bad.

In contrast, shame says I am bad. It focuses on the person. Shame is toxic. It says I am unworthy and unlovable, because of something I did, or who I am, or what was done to me by someone else. You can be shamed by anyone—parents, peers, your boyfriend, your spouse, and even, strangers. You can experience shame anywhere—in a public setting or in secret.

Imagine you are driving home from work. You are set to meet a friend for dinner. But traffic is heavy, and you know you are going to be late for your reservation. You grab your phone out of your purse to send a short text message to your friend. You hit the send button and then you look up. Too late, you brake hard but still manage to hit the car in front of you that had stopped quickly due to the traffic.

If you feel guilt, you say, "Oh my goodness! I know better than to text and drive. This is probably going to cost me a fortune and make me even later for dinner!"

If you feel shame, you say, "I'm an idiot. I am obviously a horrible driver and an even more horrible person. I shouldn't even be driving!"

Guilt is about action. Shame is about the person.

Some of us are aware of our shame while others are clueless that they are indeed feeling shame. Being unaware of the shame and where it comes from, can cause a person to hide or mask the unpleasant and painful feelings of shame they are living with. Anger issues, addictions, eating disorders, or self-harm, all can be indicators of a deep wound caused by shame. Whether we are cognizant of our shame or not, we rarely talk of our shame experiences. We push them down deep inside hoping they will disappear altogether or at least lose their sting.

You can collect your shame, experience after experience, thought after thought, lie after lie. You can accumulate so much of it that it becomes a burden too heavy to bear. For many, shame makes us want to hide away from the world or even just disappear. Shame creates an ache deep in our souls and only God can take that ache away. And there is no time frame for the experience of shame—it can be short-lived or a core experience of the self—it may begin in childhood, adolescence, or adulthood.

Envision your life as a trip around the world. When you are born, you are given a suitcase to pack all the essentials you will need with just enough room left to gather important mementos from all the places you will visit. But, instead of packing light happy memories in your suitcase, you fill it full of heaviness—unhappy things, mistakes you've made, negative words, anxiety, trauma, and broken relationships. Your suitcase for your journey through life gets heavier and heavier until there is no room for joy. Instead, your suitcase is full of shame.

Bottom line: shame prevents you from embracing the truth that God loves you no matter what. Nothing could be farther from the truth! Remember, you have great value as someone He has made in His image.

What kind of shame have you packed in your suitcase, beloved?

Do you believe that He loves you no matter what you've done, seen, thought, experimented with, or even experienced? That nothing could separate you from His love? That you are His daughter, and He loves you unconditionally? That He is the ultimate source of your provision and healing? Or do you believe that might be true for others but not for you?

Do you wear a scarlet letter on your chest? Do you blame yourself and believe you are a bad person because of something you've done, a poor choice or a colossal mistake?

Do you feel that you are damaged and unlovable because you were taken advantage of and traumatized? Something that was done to you by someone else?

Do you believe you are fundamentally flawed because you don't measure up to society's ideal of perfection or beauty?

Our shame may be the result of sin, or it may not. It doesn't matter, you can unpack your suitcase. The Bible is full of examples of individuals who did just that. Women and men who made mistakes, bad choices, or experienced pain and trauma at the hands of someone else. Each time, God forgave—He redeemed— He restored.

Rachel stole treasures that didn't belong to her. Forgiven. Redeemed. Restored.

Miriam was jealous of her brother and thirsted for power. Forgiven. Redeemed. Restored.

King David was a liar, adulterer, and murderer. Forgiven. Redeemed. Restored.

Rahab made her living as a prostitute. Forgiven. Redeemed. Restored.

Jonah was a coward and ran from God in an act of rebellion. Forgiven. Redeemed. Restored.

The woman caught in the act of adultery. Forgiven. Redeemed. Restored.

Are we any different than these women and men? No, we are not! They were real people just like us. They lived their lives in a world full of challenges, not unlike our own. Each one possessed both strengths and weaknesses. Each one experienced failure, heartache, and betrayal of some kind. Each one wrestled with the gut-wrenching shame. And we have much to learn from each of their stories—they are examples of people just like us who unpacked their suitcases.

And what about the woman with the issue of blood?

She had suffered for twelve years with constant bleeding. Can you imagine having a period for that long? She had been to every doctor and healer seeking relief. No one could help her. What makes her condition worse is that she was considered to be "unclean" by society's standards. People avoided her and whispered about her "uncleanliness" when she walked by. Think of how she must have felt? Weak, Hopeless, Alone, Ashamed. After so many years, she only knew herself as a dirty and unwanted woman.

I'm sure she had reached many a breaking point, I know I would have. But she wasn't willing to give up yet. She dug deep inside and found the courage to step out in faith. She believed that her life could be different but only with Jesus's help.

She made a life-altering choice. She took her burden to the only one who could heal and make her whole again. She pushed through the crowd that had gathered around Jesus. She believed if she could just get close enough to Jesus, she would be saved. She was right! When she touched the hem of Jesus's robe, her bleeding stopped immediately.

"Who touched me?" Jesus asked. Everyone denied it, and Peter said, "Master, this whole crowd is pressing up against you. But Jesus said, "Someone deliberately touched me, for I felt healing power go out from me." When the woman realized that she could not stay hidden, she began to tremble and fell to her knees in front of him. The whole crowd heard her explain why she had touched him and that she had been immediately healed. "Daughter," he said to her, "your faith has made you well. Go in peace."

Luke 8:45-48

Whatever fills your suitcase, right here and right now, you can begin to unpack it, leaving your shame behind, just like the woman with the issue of blood.

First, recognize that you are not your sin, nor are you what others have done to you. Allow God to renew your heart and mind with His grace, mercy, and love.

Sin is no longer your master...you live under the freedom of God's grace.

Romans 6:14

Second, accept you cannot change what you did or what happened to you. You can't have a redo, take back, or erase. It is in the past. Gone. Don't look back.

> *Forget all that—it is nothing compared to what I am going to do. For I am about to do something new. See, I have already begun! Do you not see it? I will make a pathway through the wilderness. I will create rivers in the dry wasteland.*
>
> Isaiah 43:18-19

Third, believe that your healing is possible, understanding that it will take time.

> *He heals the brokenhearted and bandages their wounds.*
>
> Psalms 147:3

Fourth, move forward, one step at a time, expectant for your future, focusing on your relationship with Him.

> *This means that anyone who belongs to Christ has become a new person. The old life is gone; a new life has begun!*
>
> 2 Corinthians 5:17

If you need a little more reassurance that moving on is possible, consider the woman at the well. She is never named in scripture yet her encounter with the Lord is the longest between Jesus and another individual ever recorded. I believe she represents all of us in her iconic story found in John 4:1-28.

The Samaritan woman is very much like many of us. I am positive that she believed she was unworthy of love. She has had five husbands, a string of broken relationships, and is currently living with another man. This woman was looking for her value everywhere but the right place. She had obviously experienced rejection, hurt, and perhaps even betrayal in her relationships with men.

She was also a social outcast—despised and rejected by everyone around her. I can just hear the other women in the village referring to her as "that awful woman" in hushed tones as she walked by. Even more, she was unaware of her role as God's beloved daughter. She was carrying a very heavy suitcase, full of shame when she met Jesus Christ that day at the well.

Because of her encounter with Christ, she was able to unpack her shame and understood that her past life and actions, while awful and devastating, didn't make her a bad woman. She had made many mistakes, done awful things, and made bad decisions, but she wasn't a mistake, she wasn't an awful person, and she was not bad! She was the daughter of the King. Broken and desperate, she cried out for forgiveness. And she was forgiven, redeemed, and restored.

Experiencing a big dose of guilt for her actions was entirely appropriate. Believing that what she had done had somehow disqualified her from living a life of victory would not be appropriate. She owned her past and all that it contained. She repented and moved forward into her future, not looking back. She accepted the love, truth, and redemption that was offered to her. She unpacked her suitcase.

God cares for us so much that He sent his son right into the middle of the hot mess of humanity. And only through the blood of Jesus, can we clean our beautiful, fragile, mucked up, and crazy lives.

And on my journey to find what my soul longed for, that's what I did! I opened my suitcase and I dumped out everything that was in it. I unpacked it all. I emptied the shame that I had been carrying, about my failed marriage, keeping my daughters in an abusive home for too long, my inability to fix my life, my lack of trust in God, and so much more. I left it all behind at the well just like the Samaritan woman did. I gave it to Him. And He took it all away. My suitcase isn't heavy anymore. Instead of dragging it behind me, I can run with it now, straight into the future God has planned for me. You can too.

It's time to recognize that holding on to your shame is very destructive to your relationship with God. The enemy of our heart wants you to feel like you are an outcast, a failure and unlovable. When you feel that way, it keeps you from confidently approaching your Father's throne. It puts a wedge between you and God. Intimacy is impossible if there is a brick wall standing in the way.

> *"If I had not confessed the sin in my heart, the Lord would not have listened."*
>
> Psalms 66:18

You are no longer the same person who made a mistake, who messed it up, failed someone, or experienced trauma. Instead of choosing shame, choose to believe God's promise of grace and mercy. You must forgive yourself. Ignore the lies. Don't feed them. If your shame is in the depths of the sea, as far as God is concerned, why are you still holding on to it? There are many chapters left to write in the beautiful story of your life. Behold you are a new creation—all things are new.

Don't wait another moment, beloved, to start unpacking your suitcase.

Ask Tough Questions

Do I believe in God?

I have asked myself this question on more than one occasion. When I look at the incredible nature all around me: I say yes! When I share my testimony: I say yes! When I consider what He has done for me, mine, and others: I say yes! When I reflect on His Word: I say yes! When I experience blessings and miracles: I say yes! I believe in God. I believe His Word is truth. I believe God's Son, Jesus Christ, is the savior of the world. I believe in the comfort and gifts of the Holy Spirit. I live for Him. I'm all in! But, if I'm being honest, am I really all in? All the time? No matter what?

I came across a term in a book written by Craig Groeschel, *The Christian Atheist: Believing in God but Living as if He Doesn't Exist*, while I was researching and preparing a lecture for one of my classes. At first glance, it didn't make much sense. *Christian Atheist*. But, as I continued to read, the reality of it hit me like a ton of bricks.

What is a Christian Atheist? *Someone who believes in God, yet lives as though He doesn't exist.*

Talk about a gut punch! This term hit a little too close to home. I knew I believed in God; but did I really live my life in a way that left no question about my belief? Did I believe it all, everything little thing He said in His Word? Or did I have doubts that God's promises were for me?

These are tough questions to ask yourself. They are even more challenging to answer. Believe me. This exercise in fearless questioning requires you to let your guard down. The tough questions lead to equally tough answers that in all honesty, you might be afraid to hear. Becoming 100% vulnerable with yourself is no easy task! But, before you can get any closer to what your soul longs for, you must take the time to wrestle with these questions and answers.

It's a "words versus actions" paradigm. You can say you believe in God, but does your life reflect this belief beyond a shadow of a doubt? For example, I believe in God, but do I believe that I am fearfully and wonderfully made? If my answer is yes, then I would live my life without being plagued with feelings of inadequacy. Yes, I told you it would be challenging.

Asking and answering tough questions is not for the faint of heart. It will require you to be fearless. But

I promise you will be the better for it—stronger, more confident, and assured. I know when I wrestled with these questions and answered truthfully for myself, I have never been the same since.

To gain some perspective, let's look at the life of Eve, the first woman.

Eve had a perfect life! According to Genesis Chapter 2, she lived in the perfect place, Paradise. She had a relationship with the perfect man, Adam. Her every need was provided for by her Creator, God. And yet, she wanted the one thing she couldn't and shouldn't have—the fruit from the tree of knowledge of good and evil. Why? Because she allowed herself to be deceived by the devil, otherwise known as the serpent.

In her defense, Eve had no prior knowledge of evil so how could she discern the serpent's motivations? However, she did know what God had asked of her—she wasn't to eat the fruit from the tree. This was the only rule she had to follow. She understood she was to obey His commands. But she chose instead to give in to the temptation that was triggered by the words of the serpent. She followed her own guidance and desire and not that of God.

The serpent was the shrewdest of all the wild animals the Lord God had made. One day he asked the woman, "Did God really say you must not eat the fruit from any of the trees in the garden?"

"Of course, we may eat fruit from the trees in the garden," the woman replied. "It's only the fruit from the tree in the middle of the garden that we are not allowed to eat. God said, 'You must not eat it or even touch it; if you do, you will die.'"

"You won't die!" the serpent replied to the woman. "God knows that your eyes will be opened as soon as you eat it, and you will be like God, knowing both good and evil."

The woman was convinced. She saw that the tree was beautiful, and its fruit looked delicious, and she wanted the wisdom it would give her. So, she took some of the fruit and ate it. Then she gave some to her husband, who was with her, and he ate it, too. At that moment their eyes were opened, and they suddenly felt shame.

Genesis 3: 1-7

Eve is the perfect example of the modern-day Christian Atheist. Yes, she believed in God, but she decided to live her life as if He didn't exist. She chose her own way instead of God's way. She believed in Him. She walked and talked with her Creator. She knew Him. And yet, she doubted Him and His goodness. She didn't completely trust that His words were true. Eve is a picture of what "believing in God yet doubting His love" can do to all of us.

Tough Question #1: Do I believe in God?

Believing is only the first part of the equation. Action must follow your decision for Him.

To believe in Him and decide to follow Him, you must know who He is. The only way I know to truly get to know someone, God included, is to passionately study them. Absolutely—Unequivocally—Irrevocably. To believe in God means you love Him dearly, you pursue Him to learn more about Him every day, you strive to do your best for Him, and through His grace, you seek to imitate Him in every thought, feeling, and deed. This question and its answer are all about the depth of your faith.

This is a hard question to ask, but it's crucial that we answer it before going on to any other.

> *O God, you are my God; I earnestly search for you.*
> *My soul thirsts for you; my whole body longs for you*
> *in this parched and weary land where there is no*
> *water.*
>
> Psalms 63:1

Tough Question #2: Do I spend time with God?

God wants a close relationship with you. Relationships take time, energy, and effort—your time, energy, and effort! He wants to be your confidante, your best friend, and your source of knowledge and direction. He also wants you to just spend time in His presence so you can be renewed and strengthened in your soul and spirit. When you love someone, you spend time with them—lots of time. We need a consistent conversation with our Creator.

> *Remain in me, and I will remain in you. For a branch cannot produce fruit if it is severed from the vine, and you cannot be fruitful unless you remain in me. Yes, I am the vine; you are the branches. Those who remain in me, and I in them, will produce much fruit. For apart from me you can do nothing. Anyone who does not remain in me is thrown away like a useless branch and withers. Such branches are gathered into a pile to be burned. But if you remain in me and my words remain in you, you may ask for anything you want, and it will be granted!*
> John 15:4-7

Is your priority a relationship with Him or someone else? Who or what are you pursuing instead of God? What excuses do you make for not spending time with God? Work? Family? Fatigue? Awkwardness, because you don't know how to talk with Him?

But when you pray, go away by yourself, shut the door behind you, and pray to your Father in private. Then your Father, who sees everything, will reward you.

Matthew 6:6

Tough Question #3: Do I accept God's love?

God is love. It is His nature to love. Love is the character of God. He loves you completely, perfectly, unconditionally, without ceasing. He loved you so much that He sent His son, Jesus Christ, to earth so that you could be saved. You might believe that God loves you, but do you accept His love without question?

Do you believe that you have to earn His love? Because you don't! You are loved because you are His. And when we love God and accept His love in return, we learn how to love as He loves.

See, how very much our Father loves us, for he calls us his children, and that is what we are!

I John 3:1

Tough Question #4: Do I read God's word and accept it as truth?

The Holy Bible is the inspired word of God. It is complete and unrefutably true. God's word is our absolute authority. Pinterest scripture boards, faith quotes, inspirational YouTube videos, or any faith-based post on social media can never replace the foundational truths of the Bible. Go to the source.

Do you read the Bible? Have you hidden His word in your heart? Do you seek His guidance and wisdom found in scripture when making decisions for your life? Do you allow His word to shape your will and decisions?

> *Make them holy by your truth; teach them your word, which is truth.*
>
> John 17:17

Touch Question #5: Do I trust Him and believe He has my best interest at heart?

Bad things shouldn't happen to good people, right? I'm doing what's right but still, negative things happen to me. The truth is bad things will happen because we live in a fallen world. And I know this truth—because it is very real to me—His grace is sufficient for each day that I live—good or bad. God's favor does not prevent my suffering and yet it helps me become an overcomer. God is not going to fix every challenge in my life because He equipped me with power through Him to conquer each challenge.

Whatever is happening in my life, it doesn't mean God doesn't love me. Whatever God is doing in my life, it does not mean He doesn't love me!

> *In his kindness God called you to share in his eternal glory by means of Christ Jesus. So, after you have suffered a little while, he will restore, support, and strengthen you, and he will place you on a firm foundation.*
>
> 1 Peter 5:10

Tough Question #6: Do I shine God's love and light into others' lives?

If I share my faith, will I lose a friend? A boyfriend? A husband? A family member? Am I afraid I will sound stupid? Or I won't do it correctly? Perhaps, you are overthinking it. Sharing your faith with someone doesn't require you to give a message that is perfectly prepared, academically rigorous, or incredibly exciting. Sharing your faith is about being honest about your journey with God.

The best way to share your faith is to share your story. Your story is powerful, and it can serve as an inspiration to others. Simply share your journey!

> *For you are to be his witness, telling everyone what you have seen and heard.*
>
> Acts 22:15

Tough Question #7: Do I pursue Him in a community of believers?

Being a part of a healthy vibrant community of faith where I am challenged and taught is elemental in my life as a believer. This journey to what our soul longs for was never meant to be done on our own. We were created for relationships with others. This truth explains our desire for connection, friendship, and intimacy. And we need those relationships to be with like-minded individuals. Engaging, along the way, with others who are also traveling, strengthens you and empowers you.

Being a part of a community will give you a sense of belonging. It will give you a community that will help you stay accountable to Him.

> Let us think of ways to motivate one another to acts of love and good works. And let us not neglect our meeting together, as some people do, but encourage one another, especially now that the day of his return is drawing near.
>
> Hebrews 10:24-25

Tough Question #8: Do I pursue a life of purity with my mind, my heart, and my body?

Pursuing purity in all things often gets a bad rap. Isn't purity an archaic concept? No, it is not. The pursuit of purity brings us closer to God and to the person He has designed us to be. If I say I am pure, I am pursuing a lifestyle that is free from anything that would contaminate, pollute, debase, or distort my mind, heart, and body. Purity requires us to be single-minded and focused. Purity leads to clarity, not confusion. Purity means I am living a life free from anything or anyone that might impede my development, my purpose and calling, and my relationship with God.

The mind leads every feeling and action that we have. Pursuing purity of the mind requires us to replace impure thoughts with Christ-like thoughts. What are you filling your mind with? What are you watching, reading, listening to, or interacting with on the internet? Is there anything you are thinking, feeling, or doing that you would not want also to think, feel, or do if you were in the presence of God? Examine your mind.

> *Your eye (mind) is like a lamp that provides light*
> *for your body. When your eye is healthy, you whole*
> *body is filled with light. But when it is unhealthy,*
> *your body is filled with darkness.*
>
> Luke 11: 34-35

The heart is the seat of our emotions. Pursuing purity of the heart requires us to recognize our selfish desires and motivations and exchange them for those that are based on godly intentions. Do you think of yourself first? Do you love other things or other people more than you love God? Examine your heart.

Come close to God, and God will come close to you.
Wash your hands, you sinners; purify your hearts,
for your loyalty is divided between God and the
world.

James 4:8

The body was created by God and given to us as a gift. Pursuing purity of the body requires us to care for our bodies keeping them healthy, whole, and free from toxins. Yes, this is all about doing things that make our bodies strong and healthy, like eating well and exercising. It also means that we strive to keep our bodies free from sexual immorality, substance abuse, eating disorders, and any other risk-taking behavior. Examine your body.

Don't you realize that your bodies are actually
parts of Christ? Should a man take his body, which
is part of Christ, and join it to a prostitute? Never!
And don't you realize that if a man joins himself to
a prostitute, he becomes one body with her? For the
Scriptures say, "The two are united into one." But
the person who is joined to the Lord is one spirit with
him. Run from sexual sin! No other sin so clearly
affects the body as this one does. For sexual immo-
rality is a sin against your own body. Don't you re-
alize that your body is the temple of the Holy Spirit,

*who lives in you and was given to you by God? You
do not belong to yourself, for God bought you with a
high price. So you must honor God with your body.*

I Corinthians 6:15-20

Tough Question #9: Do I change my values based on circumstance?

Your core values form the very foundation of your life. Values are principles and standards by which you live every day. Your values influence every choice you make. Your values impact every relationship you have. Your values inform every career decision you make. Your values have the power to strengthen you if they remain consistent and grounded in scripture. Values also have the power to weaken your position in life if they are easily changed or rooted in cultural messages.

Your values need to reflect biblical values: love, life, generosity, courage, truth, forgiveness, humility, respect, hope, peace, knowledge, wisdom, relationships, purity, faith, prayer, dignity, service to others, sacrifice, and gratitude. These biblical values illustrate the ways in which we would love for others to treat us, right?

*Do to others whatever you would like them to do to
you. This is the essence of all that is taught in the
law and the prophets.*

Matthew 7:12

Think about the world around you. Reflect on the messages that culture is sending you. Is there anything in culture today that is in direct opposition to what God values? Is there anything you are thinking, doing, feeling, or saying that disagrees with God's values? What you value needs to become what He values.

Tough Question #10: Is there anyone in my life that I have not forgiven for hurting me?

This is a tough one to ask and answer. Of course, you have been hurt by the words or actions of another person. And you have surely experienced some wounds, whether physical and/or psychological, that continue to fester. You may be dealing with feelings of anger, bitterness, vengeance and even hate as a result of the transgression against you. If you fit into any of these categories, it's time to forgive.

Forgiveness is a psychological process of the mind and heart that takes time and determination. It is you making a decision to let go of your pain, resentment, and grudges. Forgiving another person doesn't mean that you are forgetting or excusing their behavior, including the hurt or harm they have brought to you. Nothing will ever change the past. But forgiveness can loosen the past's hold on your life. Forgiving another person makes you stronger, gives you peace and joy, and moves you forward.

Make allowance for each other's faults and forgive anyone who offends you. Remember, the Lord forgave you, so you must forgive others.

Colossians 3:13

Forgiveness is not really for the other person, it's for you.

Tough Question #11: Do I believe that Satan is an atheist?

Our enemy knows there is a God. He believes in God. He understands the power and supremacy of God. He is not an atheist! But the enemy neither loves God nor serves Him. He hates God and everything good that He is.

You say you have faith, for you believe that there is one God. Good for you! Even the demons believe this, and they tremble in terror.

James 2:19

He also knows that he will ultimately have to give account to God for his actions. At the end of time, Satan will be bound forever and cast into hell. In fact, Jesus Christ has already defeated him when He died on the cross and rose again.

He canceled the record of the charges against us and took it away by nailing it to the cross. In this way, he disarmed the spiritual rulers and authorities. He shamed them publicly by his victory over them on the cross.

Colossians 2:13-15

Yet, Satan, our enemy, continues to rebel and try to destroy God's creation—us.

I know this is tough to hear. I also know that I risk you throwing this book against a wall or into the nearest trash can! It's so tough, so vulnerable; so challenging. I also know that it's God's truth. We have to ask these questions, wrestle with the answers, challenge ourselves, and look deep within. Allow Him to guide you, empower you and sustain you with His love and His word.

His grace is sufficient, beloved. It's time to ask the tough questions.

Let Down Your Hair

"Rapunzel, Rapunzel, let down your hair!"

This is my favorite line from this popular fairytale written by the Brothers Grimm. Who doesn't love a princess? You know the story. Rapunzel has been trapped in a tower for years by an evil witch. This tower has no door in or out. Rapunzel spends her days sitting in her room high above the world below just looking down from her window. She has every comfort she could want—food, water, clothing, a roof over her head, and surely some great books to read to pass the time—she wants for nothing— except to be happy. So, what does she do? She decides to change her circumstance. She lets down her hair, climbs down from her tower, and rides off into the sunset to live a happy life.

For a time in my life, I was Rapunzel—except for a few important details. First, my tower wasn't an actual physical building made from mortar and stone. It was a stronghold of the mind built from distorted thoughts and fears. Second, instead of trying to escape from my tower, I wanted to find a way to stay inside it. Believe it or not, I was comfortable passing each day of my life held captive in a sweet little tower room. It was a familiar safe place. I was protected there, or so I thought. Third, it wasn't an evil witch who was holding me, prisoner, I was doing that all by myself. I was my very own jailor.

Much like a medieval castle tower in a fantasy novel, I had built my stronghold as a defensive fortification. However, castle towers and strongholds of the mind do not serve the same purpose. In *The Two Towers*, a book written by J.R.R. Tolkien as part of his *Lord of the Rings* trilogy, there are two spectacular towers. One stands in Helm's Deep, a place of protection and peace, for the people of Rohan. When the people of Rohan are facing an attack on all sides, they run to Helm's Deep. It is a fortress built into the side of a great mountain. It is here they will make their stand against the evil Orc army. Helm's Deep is a tower of protection from the battle raging outside its walls.

The other tower is in Mordor, a dark powerful place full of fear and destruction. It is controlled by the evil villain Sauron. From inside this tower, Sauron and his army wage war on the good people of Middle Earth. The stronghold of the mind that I was trapped in was very much like Sauron's tower in Mordor. It wasn't a place that protected me. Instead, it was a place that invited evil inside it to live in the form of lies. And that evil almost destroyed me, and it will do the same to you if you remain its captive.

Think about it this way, the stones we use to build our towers are lies. The more we believe these lies, the more stones, the more mortar, and as a result, the higher our tower rises. The lies sound like this: *I'm no good. I'm damaged. No one will ever love me. I'm a failure. I'll never be good enough. I'm worthless.*

These statements are lies from the pit of hell! They contradict every beautiful and loving word spoken by our Father God in His word about us—His daughters. How do these lies begin? These false messages can be delivered by other people in our lives. Horrible words can be spoken over us that paralyze us with shame. Lies can also be spoken internally. We can lie to ourselves very easily. Lies that sound like a broken record, round and round these lies turn in our minds until they become all we think about.

Either way lies manipulate our minds and break our hearts. Lies can become so much a part of us, that they become truths, weaved into the very fabric of our being. And in ignoring the truth of what God says about us, we choose the lie, idolizing it to such an extreme, that we reject God's love. Your stronghold—your high tower—

is the lie that you idolize. The lie, or even lies, that has come to define you is your prison—your idol.

When I was researching this topic, I ran across a great example that explains an idol. Timothy Keller, pastor and theologian, writes in his book *Counterfeit Gods*, "What is an idol? It is anything more important to you than God, anything that absorbs your heart and imagination more than God, anything you seek to give you what only God can give." Reading this statement is not only a gut check it's a heart check of the deepest and most vulnerable kind.

You must not have any other god but me.

Exodus 20:3

In the *Large Catechism*, Martin Luther, the great theologian, priest, and hymn writer, writes that the Ten Commandments begin with a commandment against idolatry. Why is this commandment first? Well, it sets the tone for all the rest of them. Luther believed that we never break the other nine commandments without breaking the first one. I must agree with him. Idolatry is the motivation for breaking all of God's laws.

Why do we break this commandment? Is it because we are weak and sinful? I think the answer is that there is something we feel we must have, to be happy and fulfilled. Maybe that something is more important to our hearts than God Himself. We would not lie unless first, we had made something— affirmation, image, success, love, and so many others—more important and valuable to our hearts than the grace and favor of God. Idols, plain and simple, cause us to abandon God.

Idols can be anyone or anything. Idols are attractive and available. Idols are powerful and yet, elusive. They are so smooth; they can take over your life without you even being aware. And they make promises they can't keep. In my mind, the idol of perfection told me if I just worked harder at being good, the perfection I would achieve, as a result, would make me happy and fulfilled. I believed the achievement of perfection would fill the deepest longing in my heart.

I was lying to myself. It is through Him that I should seek my fulfillment, safety, and affirmation. But I believed the lie and instead looked to other things and relationships to affirm me, give me significance, and fulfillment. My idol became something I treasured more than God. And the terrible truth is that I didn't even realize that I had an idol!

How foolish are those who manufacture idols. These prized objects are really worthless.

Isaiah 44:9

So, how exactly do we build our towers? Here is the blueprint for their construction:

Lie = The Stone
Belief in the Lie = The Mortar
Lies + Belief = The Tower = The Idol

My lie (the stone) was "Susan, you will never be good enough." And I believed (the mortar) it wholeheartedly!

As a result, I spent the better part of my life trying to dispel that lie—to prove it wrong—to myself and everyone else. I became an overachiever, a relationship expert, a parenting educator, a perfectionist about my body shape, my weight, etc. My singular purpose became the achievement of perfection—it became my idol (the tower).

I spent more time thinking about perfection, striving for perfection, and beating myself up when I fell short of the target. The days became weeks then months and years until my tower, with its many stones and strong mortar rose high into the sky. The more I tried to be perfect the more insecure I became. I stressed about finding ways to be more perfect than I did about learning God's ways, talking to God, and pursuing a relationship with Him.

Wow! The insecurity that has haunted me for most of my life was rooted in the lie that I would never be good enough. My insecurity drove me to overcompensate, and I chased perfection in every area of my life. Every time I made a choice for perfection, believing the lie, instead of a relationship with God, I laid another stone in my tower. I was so focused on myself that I lost sight of everything else that was important. How glorifying to God is it if everything I think, feel, and do, simply emphasizes me?

In psychology, this self-focus or cognitive bias is known as egocentrism. When you are unable to see or understand any other perspective but your own, you are egocentric. This type of thinking will cause you to make incorrect assumptions about yourself and others, including God. When you can only see your point of view, only hear your little voice, and both are based on a lie, it's very difficult then for you to see and understand yourself as God does. You can't internalize His words of truth and His love if you are fully focused on lies and self-loathing.

> *Yes, they knew God, but they wouldn't worship him as God or even give him thanks. And they began to think up foolish ideas of what God was like. As a result, their minds because dark and confused. Claiming to be wise, they instead became utter fools. And instead of worshipping the glorious, ever-living God, they worshiped idols.*
>
> Romans 1:21-25

I must believe that I am a better example of humility and God's grace when I stop pretending that I have it all together. I am not perfect. I never will be on my own merit. In fact, I am not called to be perfect, and neither are you. We are called to be healed and as a result, we are made perfect in Him. It's not about what I do. It's about who I am. And I am a child of the Most High God. And that trumps anything I could ever do for God!

So, what about you? What lies do you believe? How high is your tower?

If you need anything or anyone more than you need a God, if you give anything or anyone more of your time and attention than you do your relationship with God, or if you have placed anything or anyone above God in your thoughts, feelings, and actions, you have an idol in your life. You are living in a tower locked in a room that you need to escape. Below is a list of some possible idols in our lives that are directly connected to the lies that have become truths in our minds.

Idol of Family

For women, family is a significant part of their lives. We love and need them, care for, and support them, and protect and provide for them. As a daughter, sister, wife, and mother, my family inhabits a great big space in my heart and in my mind. But if my love and focus in life become wholly based on my husband, my kids, and my extended family then my priorities are upside down.

My family doesn't need me to love them more. They need me to love God more because then I become the daughter, sister, wife, and mother that is the example of His love. When I love Him well, I love them well. If you prioritize your family ahead of your relationship with God, spending more time trying to meet their needs and solve their problems, you are building a tower.

Your lie might be: "My family depends on me, if I took time for other things, they would suffer."

Idol of Success

Being successful in school and in your career is certainly something you should strive for. You have been gifted with abilities and skills. You have been called to a particular work in His kingdom. God wants you to be a leader in your profession and contribute to your community. His purpose and plan for you include your impact on others for His kingdom.

But if your motivation for what you do in life is grounded in ambition, and your need to be a success is driving your decisions in life, then you have lost your focus. Working all the time or to the point of exhausting your energy, resources, and health, and perhaps your relationships will ultimately place you in a position of loss, not gain. The moment that you place your rela-

tionship with God on the back burner and instead prioritize achievement in school and career, you are building a tower.

*Your lie might be: "When I am the best, better than every-
one else, no matter what it takes to get there, I will be satisfied."*

Idol of Perfection

Setting positive goals, staying motivated, and becoming the best version of yourself are healthy pursuits.
But being the best at all costs, setting unbelievably high
standards, and refusing to accept anything short of perfect will cause you to become hyper-focused, hyper-crit-
ical, and hyper-anxious. You will face intense and debilitating emotions when it comes to making decisions or
doing what is most healthy for yourself. Why? You are
overwhelmed with stress and paralyzed to move, afraid
of not choosing the perfect path.

Perfectionism fills your heart with comparison and a
false sense of control. Longing for perfection leads you
to create images in your mind that may look awesome
but are really just distorted dreams built on lies. And
not being able to turn those dreams into reality will only
lead you to bitterness and dissatisfaction. Real people,
real relationships, and real-life will never measure up
to the perfection of your distorted dreams. If you let
perfection become your sole pursuit, you are building
a tower.

Your lie might be: "Once I have the perfect relationship, family or job, I will be happy, and my life will be easy."

Idol of Relationship

Relationships are good. But, when you idolize that relationship, thinking that it is your sole source of value, love, and life, then you will most surely experience disappointment, hurt, and even pain. You will become weary and disillusioned. Every decision, every choice you make, is directed by the idolized relationship and not by your relationship with God. You may stay in the relationship even though it is unhealthy and dangerous. You may allow the relationship to become your identity, meaning you are nothing without the relationship. Or you may leave the relationship to look for another that will be your source of all things. Know this: an incomplete and imperfect person cannot be made complete by another incomplete and imperfect person and vice versa. Only a relationship with God makes us whole. If someone else becomes the source of your happiness, hope, and trust, replacing your relationship with God, you have built a tower.

Your lie might be: "If I don't have him in my life, I will be nothing. He is the only one who loves me."

Idol of Wealth

Having money does not make you a bad person. Wanting to provide for your family and live a comfortable life doesn't mean that you are selfish. But having money or wanting money is not the same as loving money. We live in a culture that worships money and the accumulation of things. Once you have either, it's never enough, you just want more. Whatever blessings we experience in life, whether that be wealth or gifts, their value is temporary. Your money cannot buy you happiness, love, long life, peace, or joy. Only a relationship with God can provide those things.

If you place your trust in wealth instead of God, if you boast about your wealth instead of God, if you hurt or take from others to gain wealth instead of loving others as God does, if you are constantly worried about losing your wealth, if you are envious of others' wealth, if you don't support those in need with your wealth, or if you want to be noticed and celebrated by others for your wealth, then money is your idol and you are building a tower.

Your lie might be: "If I could just have more money, I would be happy."

Idol of Affirmation

Words of affirmation are positive words and messages we receive from others. To be affirmed for who we are and for all that we do, is a natural desire, especially for women. Seriously, it's a love language, one of mine in fact. But if you crave it above all else, if you are devastated when you don't receive it, or if you think it's all you need to make you happy, you have lost perspective.

Pursuing affirmation from other people puts a wide space between you and God. Constantly wanting and even requiring affirmation from others you are in a relationship with will strain the relationship and can even damage it permanently. It's funny, no matter how much affirmation you receive if it is your idol, you will never get enough to be satisfied. Believe me, I know about this idol from experience. If you depend on the words of others to determine your value rather than God's, you are building a tower.

Your lie might be: "The more approval and affirmation I receive, the greater is my value as a woman."

Idol of Image

Image is everything! Very true, if you embrace the truth that you were made in the image of God and your image reflects His love and sovereignty. If, however, your image or the image you seek to reflect is based on others or an unrealistic model of perfection, image is nothing! This Idol of Image is friends with the Idol of Perfection. Image is an idol if you find yourself struggling with the content you view on social media because everyone's life, appearance, relationships, and success, look better, bigger, and brighter than yours.

Image is an idol if you spend most of your time scrolling through Instagram, Facebook, or any other social media platform, comparing yourself to another person. Image is an idol if you are constantly trying to change your physical body to make it look like someone else or the latest cultural version of beauty. Living in this tower leaves us anxious, depressed, and feeling less than. Instead of striving to become more like the image of another, you must remember you were made in the image of God, or you are building a tower.

Your lie might be: "If I could just be the perfect size 4 like her, then my life would be amazing!"

Idol of Addiction

There is no such thing as a healthy addiction. An addiction is a chronic condition with damaging biological, psychological, social, and environmental consequences. There is also no such thing as being immune to the effects of one. No matter the source or object of the addiction: food, alcohol, drugs, sex, pornography, gambling, exercise, all addictions rewire our brains, harm our hearts, isolate us from our community, and destroy our relationship with God. An addiction to a substance or an activity will cause you to lose control over your actions, thoughts, and your feelings. If the need to satisfy your addiction is stronger than your desire for God, you are building a tower.

Your lie might be: "I know what I'm doing. I could stop any time I wanted. I've got it all under control. Besides, there is no harm in it."

Of course, this is in no way is an exhaustive list of the idols that can take over our lives. Whatever your idol, know this. Idols are empty. Idols never fulfill. Stack up enough idols in your life and you have built yourself a pretty tall tower. You've been trapped inside for too long. It's time to look your idol straight in the eye, see the lies for what they are—just lies! Dare to believe God's promises and replace the lies with His truth. We are taught in God's word to pull down idols and destroy them.

> *Therefore, my dear friends, flee from idolatry.*
> 1 Corinthians 10:14

It's time to make a choice. Only you can. You can stay a prisoner in your stronghold, or you can fight the battle to win back your mind. It's time to obliterate the idolatrous stronghold in your life. Freedom is in your reach. He's got your back! He will fight by your side. Put on the full armor of God and wage war.

> *Therefore, put on every piece of God's armor so that you will be able to resist the enemy. In the time of evil. Then after the battle you will still be standing*

firm. Stand your ground, putting on the belt of truth and body armor of God's righteousness. For shoes, put on the peace that comes from the Good News so that you will be fully prepared. In addition to all of these, hold up the shield of faith to stop the fiery arrows of the devil/ put on salvation as your helmet, and take the sword of the Spirit, which is the word of God.

Ephesians 6:13-17

Let our Father God, help you fight for your freedom. I know you are scared. I was too. Know this, He goes before you, He walks beside you, and He has got your back. You can do it. And I promise it will be worth it.

Let down your hair, beloved, and leave the lies and idols behind.

Play the Waiting Game

On your mark—Get set—Wait!

The waiting game should be familiar to all of us. It isn't a game played for the entertainment value. Neither is it a relationship game marked with manipulation, malice, or cut-throat intent. It's a game of life that we've been playing since we were kids.

Waiting for our next birthday, waiting our turn, waiting for the weekend, waiting to grow up, waiting till school is done and summer begins. When we finally leave our childhood and teen years behind and become adults, the waiting just gets more complicated. We wait for a promotion at work. We wait for that special someone to arrive. We wait for our circumstances or relationship to change. We wait to feel life stirring in our wombs. We wait for healing when we are ill. We wait for the next season in our life to arrive. Always waiting.

And I hate it! Waiting is an excruciating experience for me. My mom has always told me that even before I was born, she knew I was going to be a mover and a shaker! She was right. I am never still, and I am not one for delaying action. I am impatient and often act before I think or pray for wisdom. Feeling that eager anticipation of a reality not yet realized and having absolutely no control over the speed of the process creates the ultimate challenge for me.

Merriam Webster's Dictionary defines waiting as "staying in place until an expected event happens; until someone arrives; until it is your turn to do something: to not do something until something else happens; to remain in a state in which you expect or hope that something will happen soon."

Biblically, the Hebrew word for *waiting* is *kavah* meaning "to hope, to expect, to eagerly look for." References to waiting occur 116 times in the Bible. Both Sarah and Hannah waited a long time for a child, Joseph waited for deliverance, the people of Israel waited in the wilderness to enter the promised land, Job waited for healing, and Israel waited for a Messiah. And then there is Ruth.

She was no stranger to the waiting game. Ruth and her mother-in-law, Naomi, had suffered great losses. They were living in a time of war and great famine in the land. Both of their husbands had died, and they were left with nothing and no one, except each other. They were vulnerable and found themselves in dire straits. But, instead of Ruth going back home to her family so she could be cared for her, she commits instead to go with Naomi to her home in Bethlehem and to care for her. Talk about loyalty!

> *But Ruth replied, "Don't ask me to leave you and turn back. Wherever you go, I will go; wherever you live, I will live. Your people will be my people, and your God will be my God.*
>
> Ruth 1:16

When Ruth decides to go with Naomi, her waiting game begins. While she cares for Naomi, she waits for provision. She waits for love. She waits for a home. She waits for children. I am sure she felt frustrated and impatient at times. No doubt, she asked God why she was even in this situation in the first place. And I am confident that Ruth felt alone at times and wondered when her wait would end.

And yet, Ruth's story is one of hope and God's faithfulness to his daughter. In the final chapter, we read that Ruth's patience and perseverance in the waiting game are rewarded. She is blessed with everything she needed: a home, a husband named Boaz, a son, and a beautiful future. Her son will be the grandfather of King

David and in the lineage of Jesus Christ. She played the waiting game well.

I guess you could say it's a foregone conclusion that you will experience seasons of waiting in your life. Yes, you will feel restless, nervous, or maybe even frustrated while you wait. I've never met anyone who enjoys delayed gratification. We want to see the Lord answer our prayers immediately! We want provision now. We want healing now. We want His favor and blessing now. We want to be rescued now. We are an impatient lot to be sure.

How did I play the waiting game? Not very well at first but I did finally get the hang of it.

As I began my journey to what my soul longed for, I still didn't understand the path my life had taken, the pain, the heartache, the devastation that was my life before I got out of my boat. I struggled to make sense of it all. Through God's grace and the foundation that was built in my life as a child by my parents to lean into God when I am troubled, I kept going. It wasn't easy. I wanted to give up more times than I can count. But I remained faithful in the face of this overwhelming tragedy that was my life because I simply didn't know what else to do.

But as I pressed forward into the waiting game, I became impatient. I was a middle-aged mom tired of being still, waiting for my blessing, my miracle. Life had thrown me a tremendous curveball. And I was 100% in my feelings at this point. Logic, rational thinking, or even a measure of common sense was nowhere to be found. I felt like I was living my life in the in-between. In between my current situation and my dream scenario. In between my failed relationship and the future of a forever relationship. In between the last promise God fulfilled in my life and one I was anxiously waiting for Him to complete. Maybe you can relate to this, maybe you can't, but the in-between is where I found myself.

The in-between is all about trying. Trying to figure it all out. Trying to find God's will for my life and for my relationships. Trying to understand men. Trying to wait. Trying to be patient. Trying not to lose hope that my miracle is out there. Trying to hold on to my faith in relationships, in marriage, and in love for that matter. And this trying puts you on a non-stop rollercoaster of emotion—up and down, fast and slow, twists and turns—until you are dizzy and discombobulated with so many feelings, you lose perspective. If you want to be successful in playing the waiting game, you must get off the rollercoaster! If you don't, you will lose the game. So, stop trying and leave the in-between behind. Start waiting and looking toward your victory at the finish line.

Wait for the Lord, be strong and take heart and wait for the Lord.

Psalms 127:14

I had this deep revelation in my heart early one morning. My girls were still asleep, and the house was quiet. I was sitting alone in my favorite chair, watching the sunrise, and drinking my coffee. I picked up my Bible to read and when I opened it, this is the passage that drew my eye.

> *Take delight in the Lord, and he will give you your heart's desires.*
>
> Psalms 37:4

Weird, you hear about stuff like this happening but never imagine it will happen to you! I had read this scripture hundreds of times. But, that morning, I saw it differently and perhaps for the first time correctly. I had always focused on the latter part of the scripture— and He will give you the desires of your heart. But, if you only latch onto the second part of the sentence, believing that God will just give you what you want when you want it because you are His, then you miss the entire point of this scripture altogether. Before He will give you the desires of your heart, you must first take delight in Him.

Other translations of this passage offer us even more clarity:

Make God the utmost delight and pleasure of your life, and he will provide for you what you desire the most. (TPT)

Commit your way to the Lord; trust in him, and He will act. (ESV)

Commit everything you do to the LORD. Trust him, and he will help you. (NLT)

Delight equals commitment. When you take delight in the Lord, you are wholeheartedly, passionately, and steadfastly pledging your devotion to Him. You are choosing to commit your whole self, your thoughts, emotions, and actions to Him.

I suddenly understood how to play the waiting game. I needed to delight in Him first and as a result, the desires of my heart could be shaped and ultimately fulfilled by Him. I now know that it's during the waiting game that God does some of His best work in our hearts and lives. We don't always see the plan or understand the purpose until the game is done, but God is molding, shaping, and refining us during the wait. His goals become our goals for our life.

Don't mistake the waiting as a passive process. Waiting on God is full of action. When we are waiting, we can be proactive in building a deeper and more intimate relationship with Him. And priceless treasures can be found as we actively wait.

That very morning, I committed myself to the active process of waiting. I decided to dedicate each day to a passionate pursuit of intimacy with God. He is the source and the only one who can give me the desires of my heart. I made a choice to delight in Him and to leave the fulfillment of the desires of my heart up to Him. For the first time, I began playing the waiting game with a sound strategy.

Now, a game is only as good as its rules, and to play the game well we must follow those rules. Here are the rules as I learned them:

Rule #1: Style Your Specifics

What are the desires of your heart? Make a list.

The desire of my heart was to be married to a man who loved well—God, me, and then my girls, in that order. I wanted to experience a healthy, positive, and affirming marital relationship. I wanted to share my life with a true partner. I wanted loyalty, romance, laughter, and true commitment. My girls always joked with me that what I was looking for was a "Hallmark man!" They weren't very far from the truth.

So, I wrote an actual pen and paper list—a detailed, very specific list of the qualities I desired in my future husband as well as the blessings and healing I desired for my life. I was vulnerable and held nothing back. I prayed over my list, making my specific requests, and then I acknowledged that what God wanted for me was truly what I wanted for myself. I decided that if His list was different from mine, then I wanted what He wanted for me, even if that was to remain single. I trusted in His promise that He knew what was best for me. He is my Father after all. I put all my eggs in the same basket, His basket, and I recited these two scriptures, one in Proverbs and the other in Romans.

You can make many plans, but the Lord's purpose will prevail.

Proverbs 19:21

And we know that God causes everything to work together for the good of those who love God and are called according to his purpose for them.

Romans 8:28

Then I stuck my list in my Bible and promised to not look at it again.

Rule #2: Seek Your Treasure

How do you find the treasure? Delight in Him.

Each day I played the waiting game, I dedicated portions of my time to worship and praise, reading scripture and learning about God's promises, talking with God, and listening in return, spending time in the great outdoors marveling at God's creation, and focusing on others' needs instead of my own.

> *But if we look forward to something we don't have,*
> *we must wait patiently and confidently.*
>
> Romans 8:25

Then, I took all the many things I was learning each day and began to apply them to my life. I was committed to living a life where a relationship with God was the first thing on my mind when I woke up and the last thing on my mind when I went to sleep. He became my priority. The more I fell in love with the Lord and the more I knew Him, the more I knew what I desired in a future mate and what I did not. It was an amazing part of my journey where I was standing on the promises of God and experiencing His blessing in His time.

Rule #3: Shift Your Clock

When will my waiting be over? In God's time.

God has ordained our lives and the time we spend living them. His timing is perfect; ours is not. God is patient; we are not. God sees the big picture; we only see the small details. He doesn't use a clock to mark the passage of time like we do. His schedule for giving us the desires of our hearts is not based on minutes, hours, days, weeks, months, or even years. His timing is beyond our comprehension. We need to shift our clock from one that marks the passage of time to one that marks the practice of trust in God.

> *There is an appointed time for everything. And there is a time for every event under heaven.*
>
> Ecclesiastes 3:1

God didn't create the waiting game to manipulate, punish, hurt, or ignore us. He created it for our benefit. The goal of the waiting game is for the player to develop a greater depth of trust in the maker of the game. Seasons of waiting give us time to prepare for what is ahead, to heal from what is behind, and to become who we were designed to be—trusting Him along the way.

Rule #4: Stay Your Course

How do you finish the game well? Practice being steadfast.

> *So, let's not get tired of doing what is good. At just the right time we will reap a harvest of blessing if we don't give up.*
>
> Galatians 6:9

Don't settle. Don't compromise. Don't withdraw from others. I spent time with friends and family. I even went on a few dates. Still, things never clicked. If I did see a red flag, I quickly removed myself from the situation. I also didn't go out with everyone who asked or was nice to me. I continued to delight in Him even when I didn't feel like it. I prayed even when I felt hopeless. I talked to Him even if I didn't think He was listening. I studied His Word even when the principles I found there were challenging and sometimes difficult to hear. I practiced patience and when I would fail, as I surely did on many occasions, I didn't give up. I waited. And I played by the rules.

But God says, *"Wait, my beloved daughter. I am working on your behalf. Deep breaths, slowly, in and out. Watch and see what I will do."*

Then out of nowhere, it happened, I arrived at the final space on the game board. When I least expected it, God surprised and blessed me with the most wonderful man I have ever known—on a blind date, no less! God is an extraordinary matchmaker if you will allow Him to be one. This man, who was truly a gift from God, checked every box on my very specific list. Even better, my future husband, fulfilled desires that had been shaped by God and written by Him in my heart, while I was waiting. God knew best. He really did bring me my very own Hallmark man!

I do have one cautionary note to share. If you avoid playing the game or leave before it is finished, and instead take matters into your own hands, you are setting yourself up for disappointment. In my experience, when I get out ahead of God, to follow a plan of my own making, I am always unsatisfied with the results. It never turns out as I had planned. It's never as good as it could have been if I had just been patient.

As Dr. John Piper, pastor and author, so eloquently writes in his book, *Future Grace: The Purifying Power of the Promises of God*, "Waiting on the Lord is the opposite of running ahead of the Lord, and it's the opposite of bailing out on the Lord. It's staying at your appointed place while He says stay, or it's going at His appointed pace while he says go. It's not impetuous, and it's not despairing. We have the choice, then, to take a deep breath, release our clenched hands, and let God be God."

It's difficult to wait but more difficult to regret. Our Father does know best. Delight in Him while you wait on Him to act— to deliver, to answer your prayers, to renew your strength, to do what only God can do. His timing is not ours, but His promises are.

Trust me on this one, beloved. Play the waiting game and prepare to be amazed.

Watch Out for Traps

Mice, ugh! They are ordinary and quite small. And yet, the combination of their beady black eyes, wormy tails, sharp teeth, and twitchy movements is not only disconcerting, but it's also downright, creepy. A while back, I had a pesky mouse in our house. So, I plotted and strategized about how to catch the mouse. I set up traps in the kitchen to do the deed. I baited the trap with something the mouse dearly loves and can't pass up, cheese. I retired for the evening confident that in the morning, the mouse would be trapped.

Unfortunately, I had to get up in the middle of the night to get a drink of water. You know where this is going, right? It was dark—I couldn't see very well through my sleepy eyes, so I wasn't watching where I was going. The traps I had set were obviously not in the front of my mind and herein was the problem. Because I wasn't thinking about the traps I had set, I was the one who paid the price, not the mouse. OUCH! My toe still hurts just thinking about it.

My run-in with the mousetrap is a good illustration of what I like to call, relationship traps, and how they operate in our lives. They are the relationships we encounter along our journey that can at the very least slow us down, or at the very worst, stop us dead in our tracks, and we are unable to wrestle free from them. These relationship traps can be painful and will try to break us.

> No one can predict misfortune. Like fish caught in a cruel net or birds in a trap. So men and women are caught. By accidents evil and sudden.
>
> Ecclesiastes 9:12

Relationship traps are everywhere. Some you see if you are intentionally looking for them, walking through life confidently with caution. If you know where to look—If you know what they look like—they are easy to navigate around and avoid altogether. However, there are many relationship traps that you can't see because they are hidden so well. Sometimes they are right there in front of us, but we miss them because our focus is on something else. As a result, we are ensnared. Unfortunately, for most of us, we are caught securely in the trap without even knowing it. You wake up one morning and are surprised to comprehend that your life is no longer your own.

Why are relationship traps so easy for us to fall into? It's because one of our deepest longings is to love and be loved by someone. We all share this desire to experience a love that is pure, accepting, and overwhelming. We are driven, even recklessly at times, in the deepest parts of our souls to belong. God created us this way. He made us for relationship with Him first and others second. He gave us these desires, these longings. We want love, passion, adventure, touch, encouragement, support, trust, loyalty, fun, legacy, memories, and dreams of the future.

Both men and women are created with these desires—they may be expressed differently, but, on some level, we are both looking for each other. We are relational—God is relational. We were made for it. But we have our relationship priorities out of order. Our relationship with God comes first. Our relationship with another person comes second. We have inverted this order in our pursuit of relationship. We look to others to satisfy and fulfill us when only God can do that. I think we might all have lost perspective of this somewhere along life's journey.

Think about the mouse. What gets him to come close? What attracts him? What makes him forget any sense of danger? The Cheese! His hunger and his curiosity, both powerful experiences, when combined lure him in and ultimately, he is trapped. A relationship trap operates in the same way.

It is a snare that seduces you, through your ravenous hunger for something or someone, along with your insatiable curiosity, into one of two mindsets: *submission* or *control*. Our mindset is one of submission if we can no longer be true to who we are or do what we want to do because we have been brought under the control of something or someone else. When our desire is to have complete influence or authority over something or someone, we are seeking to have control. Something can be anything. Someone can be anyone.

If your mindset is one of submission, you find yourself doing or saying things you never wanted to. You realize that the life you are living is not the life you imagined for yourself at all. You recognize too late that someone else is in control of your life when it should be you. And it's not because that someone has any true feelings for you. It's not about love; it's not about respect; it's not about friendship or relationship at all. That someone needs your submission, no matter what it takes, because that someone believes that having power and control over someone else, will bring something that is missing from their life. It is insecurity, low self-esteem, and unhappiness that drive a person's need for control. In fact, it is their inability and or failure to control their own lives that causes them to desire control over yours. Honestly, that someone who is seeking control, needing your submission, may even be you!

If your mindset is one of control, you find yourself feeling like a ship without a rudder, and the desire to take control is so strong, that you will find even the smallest thing to establish as yours and yours alone. But that small thing will soon become larger than life, wielding more power than you could have imagined. When you want something so badly that you will do anything to obtain it, the thing you want has the power, not you. Either way, the relationship trap that ensnares you will choke you and you will become someone you don't even know.

My mindset was submission. Throughout my life, I have never believed I was "all that" or that I had it "going on." The people that have those thoughts are self-absorbed. They think too much of themselves. I was just the opposite. I thought too little of myself. Sure, I covered it well. But down deep, at my core, my issue was not a struggle with superiority but a struggle with inferiority. Relationships validated me, so, I was vulnerable to a trap.

I didn't realize then what I have come to understand now. And that is that my irrational and unfounded insecurity, specifically, that I would only be validated as a worthwhile human being by being in a love relationship, blinded me from seeing the very destructive relationship trap right in front of me. I was caught—hard and fast—never knowing what hit me until much later.

I truly believed that I needed someone else to complete me—to fill the holes in my heart—the empty spots in my life. I needed someone to make me better. I was sure that the love of someone else would make me happy with myself. And guess what? I did find that someone—the wrong someone. I found myself in a very bad relationship. Sometimes, bad relationships occur because someone doesn't really love you. But in my case, I was in a relationship with someone who didn't have a loving heart. You can't be loved by someone who does not have any love to give.

You see, his mindset was one of control and I was just the type of person he needed to validate him. He reminded me daily, in every word and deed, that I was nothing without Him. Tragically, over time, sometimes in small ways, words or looks, and other times after traumatic betrayals, I believed him. Over the years of our marriage, slowly and painfully, I became a stranger to family, friends, and even to myself. I had become who I needed to be so that I could survive in the toxic relationship I was living in. I wasn't who God created me to be, I was lost.

Here's the truth I forgot: God is the only source that can fill the holes in my heart and spirit. He is the only one. Why do we look everywhere but up for the answer? Relationships should celebrate who you are not damage or tear down who you are. Healthy relationships are nurturing, and unhealthy ones are damaging. There is a popular phrase that says it best, "If life was a storybook, the person we fall in love with wouldn't be the person who broke us."

And too often, we become desensitized to the negativity and hurt we experience in a bad relationship and just accept it as if it is totally normal. We become blinded to the dysfunction in our relationship. Just like a mouse, we have poor eyesight and will follow the known route instead of risking the unknown. Just like a mouse, we become a creature of habit, craving predictability, and a sense of security. We will remain in the place we know, the unhealthy relationship we have learned to survive in because even if it's awful, there are no surprises. The predictability of the dysfunction provides us with a false sense of safety. Instead of risking the unknown and breaking free of the dysfunction, we remain, losing more of ourselves each day.

The usual ups and downs we experience in any relationship don't mean our relationship is a bad one. Every healthy relationship will encounter seasons of conflict and challenge. A toxic relationship is very different. It steals your joy, sucking the life out of you and transforms you into someone you no longer recognize.

For people will love only themselves and their money. They will be boastful and proud, scoffing at God, disobedient to their parents, and ungrateful. They will consider nothing sacred. They will be unloving and unforgiving; they will slander others and have no self-control. They will be cruel and hate what is good. They will betray their friends, be reckless, be puffed up with pride, and love pleasure rather than God. They will act religious, but they will reject the power that could make them godly. Stay away from people like that!

2 Timothy 3:1-5

Scripture gives us great clarity regarding the signs we need to look for if we want to avoid a relationship trap. People who are defined by any of the qualities listed in the passage above should trigger a warning that you don't need to ignore. Red means stop! Red flags are clear signs that a person probably can't have a healthy relationship.

The signs of an unhealthy relationship may include an unwillingness to compromise, any type of abuse (including emotional, physical and/or sexual), communicating with criticism or contempt ("putting you down"), controlling or violent behavior, lying, isolation, persistent jealousy, lack of close relationships with family or friends, withdrawal, anger issues, cheating, narcissism or a lack of intimacy and security. Red flags can appear while dating, engaged, or after marriage.

If there are one or more red flags in your relationship, ignoring them won't make them disappear. In fact, ignoring red flags is like pouring gasoline on a flame. They will only grow bigger and eventually consume the relationship. Believing that you can change a person, that your love and care will eradicate the red flags, is dangerous and in all reality, it doesn't work. A person must be aware that they need to adjust their personality, thinking, feeling, and acting. They must desire and choose to make whatever changes are required while committing to doing whatever it takes to be successful. It's up to them—not you. You cannot change a person!

Shift your focus from trying to change or save an unhealthy person with your love to trying to connect with a healthy person who will love you well. Even more so, don't settle for a relationship or being loved any less than Jesus Christ loved us.

> *So now I am giving you a new commandment: Love each other. Just as I have loved you, you should love each other.*
>
> John 13:34

> *For husbands, this means love your wives, just as Christ loved the church. He gave up his life for her to make her holy and clean, washed by the cleansing of God's word. He did this to present her to him-*

*self as a glorious church without a spot or wrinkle
or any other blemish. Instead, she will be holy and
without fault. In the same way, husbands ought to
love their wives as they love their own bodies. For a
man who loves his wife actually shows love for himself. No one hates his own body but feeds and cares
for it, just as Christ cares for the church. And we are
members of his body.*

Ephesians 5: 25-30

This charge to husbands is crystal clear. A husband,
or future husband, must love his wife sacrificially because Jesus's love for us was sacrificial. Christ gave up
everything, even His own life, for us. Husbands must
be willing to do the same for their wives. A husband
must serve his wife. To serve another person means
that you put aside your own interests for the other person's good. He loves his wife first and then himself. He
must live his life displaying a fierce commitment and
faithfulness to his wife and family. He should lead with
care and understanding. And above all, a husband must
submit himself to God, pursuing wisdom, guidance,
and an intimate relationship with His Creator through
prayer, worship, and reading of the Word.

In addition to scripture, we can also turn to experts
in the field of Marriage and Family Science for successful relationship guidance and skill-building. Drs. John

and Julie Gottman, psychologists and therapists, have been married for sixty-two years. That's no small accomplishment! To help others sustain successful and loving relationships, they have developed *The Sound Relationship House Theory*. I teach my students in Marriage and Family class, this positive approach, which includes nine components, to creating and maintaining nurturing relationships. This theory can be applied to any stage of an intimate relationship, whether you are single and considering the qualities you are looking for in a spouse or you are dating, engaged, or married.

The foundation of a Sound Relationship House is laid by building a *love map*. You must truly know your partner, inside and out. You must like each other. This can only be done by establishing a deep and abiding friendship. Asking yourself questions like, how well do I know him? His past? What worries him? What brings him happiness? What are his hopes, dreams, and aspirations? What makes him laugh? It's all in the details and learning them all takes a lifetime. Friendship is the foundation of the house, and all other levels are built upon it.

"When you choose to spend your life with someone, you hand them a map to your inner world. Your inner world is, of course, quite complex including the memories of your past, the details of your present, your hopes for the future. It includes your deepest fears and your grandest dreams. But the map you hand your partner is a pencil sketch. The task for couples is to intentionally be adding details to that map. It needs scale, direction, and a legend. Over the course of a lifetime, you will be constantly adding landmarks, texture, and color." Drs. John and Julie Gottman

Next, we must *share our fondness and admiration* with each other. Expressing appreciation, respect, and affection within your relationship facilitates positivity. Make the most of every moment, small and large, to connect with each other, *turning towards one another instead of away*. When you have episodes of disagreement, approach problem-solving using *a positive perspective*. Conflict is natural, inevitable, and quite functional if you manage that conflict appropriately.

Focus on creating an environment that encourages honesty, vulnerability, and open conversation about the things that matter, values, goals, and convictions. When you do, you are working together to *create shared meaning* in your lives and helping each other *make your dreams come true*.

What is the glue or cement that holds the house together? Trust and Commitment. When you are confident in knowing that your partner is focused on thinking about and doing what needs to be done to maximize your interest instead of his own, you can trust him. You know he will be there for you no matter what comes your way. When you and your partner believe, and this includes acting on this belief, that your relationship is forever, a lifelong journey, for better and worse, then you are resolved. That's *commitment!*

When all nine components are present, you have a well-built house that can stand strong through stresses, storms, and successes.

> *Anyone who listens to my teaching and follows it is wise, like a person who builds a house on solid rock. Though the rain comes in torrents and the floodwaters rise and the winds beat against that house, it won't collapse because it is built on bedrock.*
>
> Matthew 7:24-25

Let's consider the mouse once more. Did you know a mouse has a very sensitive sense of smell? It can easily detect the scent of the bait and that of the human setting the trap. The mouse knows the trap is there and as a result, even if tempted, will not take the bait. Did you also know that a mouse is pretty smart and even cautious? It learns to avoid the dangerous trap set for it and lives to eat another day. It also communicates with the other mice and lets them know where danger is lurking. I think we can learn some valuable lessons from the mouse when it comes to watching out for traps.

Stay alert and know that not all relationships are good for you. Take your time and don't rush into a relationship because you think it is the answer to all your problems. Be sensitive to red flags and don't ignore them. Exercise boldness, and don't settle for anything less than a bedrock relationship. Continue to learn and practice the skills that produce healthy relationships.

Beloved, keep talking to God because He will guide you away from the traps and direct your path.

Don't Be Afraid of the Dark

Can I tell you a secret? I am a scaredy-cat! I'm afraid to close my eyes in the shower. What if someone sneaks into my house? And when I open my eyes, they are standing on the other side of the shower door staring at me. Now, here is a crazy one. I'm afraid of porta-potties—you know the free-standing toilets in parks, campsites, and anywhere else for that matter. Why? Well, I'll tell you why. What if something jumps out of it and bites me?! I also check and recheck my door to make sure it's locked. I often drive back home after leaving for work to make sure I didn't leave my curling iron powered on, so my house won't burn down. And my list of ridiculous unfounded fears goes on and on. I bet you have some crazy fears as well.

From, the time we are little girls, I think the world teaches us to be fearful about all kinds of things. Strangers. Being Alone. Heights. Social Situations. Growing

Up. When we are grown, the fear stays and even continues to grow. We can be afraid of everyday life scenarios like a failure, commitment, comparison, aging, criticism, or the future. We can also experience great fear of terrible things happening to us like some type of violence, assault, abandonment, or terminal illness.

As a psychologist, I know that fear is a natural, powerful, and incredibly complex human emotion. It's that anxious feeling in your gut when you anticipate either an imagined event or a real experience. If you were to compile a list of fears that people can experience, the list would be endless. Fear can be helpful when it alerts us to danger or a real threat. However, fear left unchecked can become debilitating, causing us to withdraw from life and others. Experiencing chronic fear impairs our ability to differentiate between threat and safety. The grown-up fears that many of us experience can, unfortunately, lead to anxiety, depression, and even substance abuse.

But whatever you fear, real or imagined, it's significant because that fear is preventing you from experiencing true freedom and peace in life. Fear can drive your every waking thought, fear can be the best friend you keep close and dear, and fear can also create a chasm between you and your best life. It can prevent you from becoming who you were created to be. It can paralyze you causing you to not stand up for yourself or to make your own choices.

My deepest fear as a child was being alone in the dark. For me, the dark was a scary place to be. I couldn't go to sleep without a nightlight on in my bedroom. Just a small beam of light in the quiet dark of my room allowed me to relax and breathe easily. I slept knowing that whenever I opened my eyes, I would be able to see whatever was around me. I'm not going to lie, I am sometimes still challenged by this fear, especially when I am home alone.

Fear of the dark is a common challenge for many people. A quote from a clinical psychologist, Alicia H. Clark, puts fear in perspective. "Darkness impairs our vision, quite literally, and this is inherently uncomfortable. We aren't afraid so much of the dark as we are afraid of what is in the dark that we can't see."

Many of life's challenging circumstances can push you into profound darkness. Your vision is then impaired, you can't see your hand in front of your face, much less the space surrounding you. It's at that point the fear will set in and gripping your mind and heart. For example, when a significant relationship in your life begins to unravel or even ends, you find yourself in the dark. When you don't get the career promotion you deserve and were counting on, or you lose your job, you find yourself in the dark. When your health is threatened or a family member receives a difficult diagnosis, you find yourself in the dark. The darkness can be soul-shaking. The darkness can squeeze us so tightly, that we are transported back in time, feeling as if we are little girls again, powerless, and scared, needing someone to comfort and perhaps even rescue us.

When my girls were little, they were scared of the dark too. I would tuck them into bed every night and read a bedtime story. *You Can Give a Pig a Pancake* and *There Was an Old Lady Who Swallowed a Fly* were favorites. After the story, I would turn out the light. Sometimes, I would lie down on the floor by their beds and sing to them until they fell asleep. When I reached up both of my hands in the dark beside their beds, two tiny hands always found mine.

When we, His daughters, reach out to Him, in the dark, His hand will take ours. He loves us. He protects us. He guides us. He reassures us. We need to trust Him, so completely, that His light is the only one we will ever need. This can a tough strategy to follow, especially, when you are alone in a dark place in your life, and you can't see your way ahead.

Hagar was alone in a very dark place and was in critical need of God's light. Let's look at her story found in the Old Testament, Genesis 16: 1-14, for a moment.

> *Now Sarai, Abram's wife, had not been able to bear children for him. But she had an Egyptian servant named Hagar. So Sarai said to Abram, "The Lord*

has prevented me from having children. Go and sleep with my servant. Perhaps I can have children through her." And Abram agreed with Sarai's proposal. So Sarai, Abram's wife, took Hagar the Egyptian servant and gave her to Abram as a wife.

Hagar, which means "one that fears," was an Egyptian slave to Sarai the wife of Abraham. I love how names have so much meaning. She is a stranger in a foreign land. The Bible doesn't go into much detail about Hagar's life before she came to live in Sarai's household. However, scripture tells us that Sarai, impatient to have a child of her own and unable to do so, decided to take matters into her own hands (not the best choice in this case!). She gave Hagar to her husband Abraham. I cannot imagine how afraid Hagar must have been—how she must have struggled with her situation. Because she was a slave, she had no rights or choices in her life. Her circumstance was not of her own making. Sarai was free to do whatever she wished with Hagar.

After Hagar becomes pregnant, things get much worse for her. Sarai treats her very harshly. Hagar felt she had no choice but to run away into the wilderness. Alone, angry, and desperate, God sends an angel to Hagar with a message. Hagar realizes that she is speaking with God and that's when she gives God a name, El Roi, "the God who sees me." Hagar is the only person in the Bible who gives God a name.

She gave this name to the Lord who spoke to her:
"You are the God who sees me," for she said, "I have
now seen the One who sees me."

Genesis 16:13

We can learn much from Hagar's story of hope. No matter how dark our circumstances might be, God sees us, just like He saw Hagar. She was a slave, a foreigner, a nobody. But, not to God. She ran away from her circumstances—her darkness. But God met her in her wilderness, shining His light into her life and she was saved. Why? Because Hagar mattered to her Creator—just like you and I matter. The God who sees me, El-Roi, sees you—right where you are.

We have all at some point in our life wandered through a wilderness of darkness. And the painful and arduous journey to make it out to the other side is not a path any of us would want to walk again. But there is much we can learn when we are in the dark, about ourselves, others, and most of all about God. He is always teaching whether the classroom is dark and murky or light and shining. He gives us nuggets of gold we can only find in the darkness. Oswald Chambers said in *The Place of Help*, "Let it be understood that the darkness our Lord speaks of is not darkness caused by sin or disobedience, but rather darkness come as a discipline to the character and as the means of fuller knowledge of the Lord."

Oh, if we would just realize that God is using the dark times to grow us in my relationship with Him. He is using the darkness to correct our path placing us on the right way. Maybe we have not come to fully trust His hand in our lives? Maybe we have wandered away from His light? Maybe we are walking down a path that is not of His design or purpose? Maybe we keep walking the same road when He wants us to turn and follow another path? Or maybe we are just too paralyzed by fear to even put our feet on the path? If God desires to teach us things, we can only learn in the dark, then we will be the losers if we resist Him. Fearing the darkness and not pushing through it will only keep us from becoming our best selves.

A perfect example of how God can use the darkness to teach us something is found in the Book of Judges, chapters 6-8.

The Midianites were so cruel that the Israelites made hiding places for themselves in the mountains, caves, and strongholds. Whenever the Israelites planted their crops, marauders from Midian, Amalek, and the people of the east would attack Israel, camping in the land and destroying crops as far away as Gaza. They left the Israelites with nothing to eat, taking all the sheep, goats, cattle, and donkeys. These enemy hordes, coming with their livestock and tents, were as thick as locusts; they arrived on droves of camels too numerous to count. And they stayed until the land was stripped bare. So Israel was reduced to starvation by the Midianites.

It was a desperate circumstance for the Israelites. They were starving, oppressed, and fearful for their lives. The hero of this story, Gideon, is living in a dark land full of fear. Gideon means "great destroyer." When we first read about this man in scripture, he is anything but. Gideon is timid, scared, and doubtful. Obviously, he had forgotten the meaning of his name! While trying to hide the grain from the Midianites, the enemy, the unimaginable happened to Gideon.

An angel of the Lord appeared to him and said, "Mighty hero, the Lord is with you!"

Gideon wasn't having it! He just didn't see himself as a hero.

"Sir," Gideon replied, "if the Lord is with us, why has all this happened to us? And where are all the miracles our ancestors told us about? Didn't they

say, 'The Lord brought us up out of Egypt?' But now the Lord has abandoned us and handed us over to the Midianites."

Then the Lord turned to him and said, "Go with the strength you have, and rescue Israel from the Midianites. I am sending you!"

"But Lord," Gideon replied, "how can I rescue Israel? My clan is the weakest in the whole tribe of Manasseh, and I am the least in my entire family!"

The Lord said to him, "I will be with you. And you will destroy the Midianites as if you were fighting against one man."

God is asking Gideon to trust Him and to lead His people out of the darkness despite Gideon's doubts. But, because he is so fearful and believes himself to be so ill-equipped to meet God's challenge, Gideon decides to test God—three times. He doubted God would truly help him, so he asked God to do three things to prove that God was trustworthy. Can you imagine?!

First, Gideon asked God to accept an offering of food that he had prepared. God did as he requested. Second, Gideon asked God to soak a piece of wool fleece he had laid out with the morning dew, not on the ground, but on the fleece. Again, God did as Gideon asked. And finally, Gideon laid out the fleece again and asked God for the exact opposite to happen—the dew would soak the ground but not the fleece. God showed up every time for Gideon.

Have you ever prayed for God to give you a sign? Have you ever asked him to show you which door to walk through? And then when He does as you have requested, it's still not enough! You still doubt Him and His hand moving in your life. So, you ask for another sign and another and another. All the while, you remain in the darkness because of your fears. You refuse to believe that He can bring you out of the dark place and into the light.

Gideon's story doesn't end here. When he decides to place his trust in God and lead his people in battle, his circumstance doesn't automatically resolve or get easier. In fact, it gets a little tougher because Gideon must now put his words into action. He must push forward through his fear—through the unknown outcome—refusing to lose his trust in God's promise. God said he would defeat the enemy and so he would no matter how tough it might get.

So, Gideon gathered his troops, 32,000 warriors, and went to war. But then God told Gideon to do something odd. God said there were too many warriors and Gideon needed to get rid of some. God didn't want the Israelites to believe it was their own strength that would ultimately defeat the enemy.

God told Gideon to say, "Whoever is timid or afraid may leave this mountain and go home."

Two-thirds of Gideon's army did just that! 22,000 scared warriors went home leaving 10,000 men to fight. But God still thought Gideon's forces were too large. So, after another cull, only 300 men were left. God liked those numbers, so, Gideon and his 300 warriors went to fight. And with God's help, they defeated 135,000 Midianite warriors! As a result, the Israelites were freed from seven years of oppression.

What can we learn from Gideon's remarkable journey? If we put our trust in God, even though we might be afraid, He will lead us out of the darkness. No matter our situation, nothing can keep us from God or deter Him from using us for His glory.

We have discussed many circumstances in our lives that put us in dark places and cause us to be afraid. The fear that is found and experienced in the dark is caused by the enemy of our minds, hearts, and souls. He is a deceiver, trickster, and distracter. He is an expert at stirring up fear and using that fear against us. He wants nothing more than to destroy you and your love of God. In fact, fear is our enemy's most powerful weapon.

When I was ten years old, my grandfather, a pastor, told me a story. Because he knew I loved cowboys and stories of the Wild West, he used the tale of an outlaw named Black Bart, to explain the enemy's plan to scare me, and I have never forgotten it.

Black Bart was an outlaw who robbed over twenty Wells Fargo stagecoaches, in California, back in the late 1800s. He was a crazy character who liked to stand in the middle of the road with a flour bag over his head and his hat perched on top of that. Waving his gun in the air, Black Bart demanded money from stagecoach drivers and passengers. Before riding off into the sunset, Bart would leave a hand-written note of poetry behind with his victims. Weirdly, he never hurt a soul in any of his robberies. Why would he need to use violence, when making people believe that he would, was all it took to get them to give up their coins?

I think the enemy of our soul, Satan, runs circles around Black Bart. He knows our weaknesses in mind and heart. He will use these weaknesses to snare us in fear. He disguises that fear as worry, anxiety, or despair. These three emotions, if they control us, can alter, and distort our decision-making. Every decision we make that is based on fear can in no way line up with God's will for our lives. And in the end, we will regret and even resent every decision we make in life that is grounded in fear.

That's why, instead of giving in to our fear, we must take *captive every thought and make it obedient to Christ*, as it says in 2 Corinthians 10:5. Replace your fear with the promises of God because they will give you the strength and courage you need to never fear the dark again. When fears attack your mind and heart, fight them with His word.

He is faithful.

> *God will do this, for he is faithful to do what he says, and he has invited you into partnership with his Son, Jesus Christ our Lord.*
>
> 1 Corinthians 1:9

He loves me.

> *Such love has no fear, because perfect love expels all fear.*
>
> 1 John 4:18

He protects me.

> *But the Lord is faithful; he will strengthen you and guard you from the evil one.*
>
> 2 Thessalonians 3:3

He helps me.

> *We can say with confidence, The Lod is my helper, so I will have no fear. What can mere people do to me?*
>
> Hebrews 13:6

He gives me power.

> *We also pray that you will be strengthened with all his glorious power so you will have all the endurance and patience you need. May you be filled with joy.*
>
> Colossians 1:11

He fights for me.

> *Do not be afraid, for the Lord you God will fight for you.*
>
> Deuteronomy 3:22

He rescues me.

> *The Lord says, "I will rescue those who love me. I will protect those who trust in my name. When they call on me, I will answer; I will be with them in trouble. I will rescue and honor them.*
>
> Psalms 91:14-15

And this verse in the Book of Isaiah was my beacon of hope during a very dark time in my life.

> *Don't be afraid, for I am with you. Don't be discouraged, for I am your God. I will strengthen you*

and help you. I will hold you up with my victorious
right hand.

Isaiah 41:10

As you have read, throughout the Bible, God tells us not to fear. When you add up all the instances that God says, "do not fear," "fear not," and "be not afraid," the total count is 365. One command for every day of the year. How reassuring and empowering! You and I will never face a day that God is not with us so there is no reason to ever be afraid.

Remember, when it's dark, switch on the light, His light. In the dark, you can experience the greatest sense of God's presence in your life. The darker it is, the brighter His light is.

The light shines in the darkness, and the darkness
can never extinguish it.

John 1:5

Even in the dark, if we reach out to God, He will lead us to joy, peace, and happiness. Submit to His will. Surrender to Him. His light will illuminate your path. Take His hand. Walk with Him.

Mountains or seas, hills, or valleys, look your darkness in the face, beloved, and say, loud and clear, "I am not afraid!"

Pass the Test

My favorite season of the year is fall because it means a new school year is underway. I love everything about school, its rhythm, its environment, and its promise of a bright future for those who will apply themselves to learning. As a professor, it is my privilege to teach and challenge students every day to know more, do more, and be more.

One of the ways to keep tabs on how much students are learning is to give them a test. The purpose of a test is to determine how much a student knows and how well they can apply that knowledge to real-life situations. To earn a good grade on my exam, you must study, you must sacrifice your time and energy, making preparation for the exam a priority.

Everyone has different methods for preparing for a test and taking it. Some students begin studying weeks before the exam, taking their time reading the assigned material, digesting it, and then organizing their thoughts and memorizing certain key points. Others procrastinate, waiting until the night before the exam to cram as much as they can into their mind hoping that they can retain the information just long enough to get to the end of the test. Some students don't prepare at all, they just waltz in, with no real motivation for success, and just wing it! Others are plagued with test anxiety, they fear they are unprepared and never will be, so they avoid the test altogether. And unfortunately, there are some students who never come to class and these students end up failing because they never tried.

Life is like a classroom. You are always learning and periodically you will be asked to take a test: God's test. These exams are God's life lessons, and they are nothing like the ones we took in high school or college for that matter. This is a plain and simple truth. In the Old Testament, the Hebrew word for test is bachan. Translation: a test examines, investigates, and scrutinizes.

Fire tests the purity of silver and gold, but the Lord tests the heart.

Proverbs 17:3

A God-given test is not for Him, it is for us. And you can be sure that God will test you. You might not like it and even argue that the test is not fair, but it doesn't change the fact that God will give you a test, multiple ones. Taking one of God's tests helps us clearly see what we're made of. It teaches us about ourselves and about God. It is during the times of testing, that God reveals His sovereignty. Only by taking the test, can we truly understand the depth and breadth of our need for God in our lives. The test is part of our learning process.

A passing grade on a God-given test depends on your attitude and your willingness to learn during the testing. Will you be refined like gold by the process or become cold and hard like steel? And if we don't pass His test, guess what? He will allow us to keep taking it until we do.

The way I see it, we have two choices when it comes to God's tests. We can resist the test by complaining, having a bad attitude, feeling sorry for ourselves, or even running from it. Or we can embrace the test. We can welcome the challenge, the process, and the shaping of our hearts by His perfecting hand. Now, I won't lie to you. Some of the most challenging times in my life have occurred during one of God's tests. But the testing catapulted me forward into a new, rewarding, and joyful season in my life.

I remember a particular season in my life that I would call a journey through the wilderness. I wasn't feeling well, and it had been a while since my last checkup. After multiple tests, my physician gave me a report that wasn't what I was hoping for. Needless to say, it rocked my world! I wanted time to stand still. I wanted the reality that I was facing to disappear.

But I had no choice. I had to keep moving forward if I wanted to get better. I felt at times if I gave into my fear, it would swallow me up. I focused on doing all that I could do to be well. The rest I had to give to God. It was very difficult for me to do this. My anxiety kicked into high gear, and I had to fight to keep my feet planted on the promises of God.

Although my health crisis seemed to go on forever, it only lasted a little while. I learned that the only thing, the most important thing, I could do during my crisis was to worship God, no matter how I felt. Over the course of a few months, my perspective shifted, and I drew closer to Him. This test was exactly what I needed at the time. It prepared me for other challenges along my journey. Now, I thank God for my wilderness experience. I learned things about myself and my relationship with God I would never have known if not for God's test of my faith.

One of my favorite books of the Bible also illustrates the power as well as the purpose of God-given tests. The Book of Esther is one of only two books in the Bible that are named after women. It tells the story of an orphan, and exile, named Hadassah, who became Esther, the Queen of Persia, and protector of her people. She was an ordinary woman who was able to do extraordinary things because she passed God's tests. The story of Esther illustrates three particular tests that God will give

His daughters at some point along their journey. Let's look deeper into Esther's story and discover the God-given tests that she was given.

Let us search the empire to find beautiful young virgins for the king. Let the king appoint agents in each province to bring these beautiful young women into the royal harem at the fortress of Susa. Hegai, the king's eunuch in charge of the harem, will see that they are all given beauty treatments. After that, the young woman who most pleases the king will be made queen. This advice was very appealing to the king, so he put the plan into effect. At that time there was a Jewish man in the fortress of Susa whose name was Mordecai son of Jair. He was from the tribe of Benjamin and was a descendant of Kish and Shimei. His family had been among those who, with King Jehoiachin of Judah, had been exiled from Jerusalem to Babylon by King Nebuchadnezzar. This man had a very beautiful and lovely young cousin, Hadassah, who was also called Esther. When her father and mother died, Mordecai adopted her into his family and raised her as his own daughter.

Esther 2: 2-7

Born during a time of Israel's exile, Hadassah lost her parents at an early age. She was adopted by her cousin, Mordecai. Fortunately, Mordecai raised her well and loved her dearly teaching her the ways of God. They lived in the capital city of Susa, in Persia, which was ruled by King Xerxes. When the King needed a wife, all eligible females in the country were brought into the palace as potential brides for the great ruler. The Bible tells us that unlike the other women, who wanted to be chosen as a potential wife to the king, Hadassah tried her best to evade the king's soldiers. Eventually, she was found and taken to the palace.

She changed her name to Esther to hide her nationality and family background. The people of Israel were captives in the land of Persia. She had no control over her situation, but she made the best of it, keeping her focus on God and all that Mordecai had taught her. When the king chose Esther to be his queen, the testing began.

God Tested Esther's Heart

As a result of the king's decree, Esther, along with many other young women, was brought to the king's harem at the fortress of Susa and placed in Hegai's care. Hegai was very impressed with Esther and treated her kindly. He quickly ordered a special menu for her and provided her with beauty treatments. He also assigned her seven maids spe-

cially chosen from the king's palace, and he moved
her and her maids into the best place in the harem.

Esther 2:8-9

Can you imagine? Living in a palace? Servants to wait on your hand and foot. Daily spa treatments and the best food? For many women, I think this kind of pampering and privilege might go to their heads. But not Esther. She found favor with everyone who knew her, even the king. I don't think this would have happened if Esther had been a diva!

God created Esther giving her beauty, strength, intelligence, and bravery. He placed her in the harem of the king laying out the path to her being chosen as queen, where she would not only have the king's ear but his heart as well. And yet, she remained true to who she was and where she came from. Instead of being enamored with all the stuff around her, she focused on the people around her. Her heart was kind. Her heart was pure. And most of all her heart remained open to God.

The king's most trusted advisor, Haman, hated the Jews. He devised a sinister plot. When Haman's plan for the murder and destruction of Esther's people, the people of Israel, became known to Mordecai, the king's scribe, she was positioned at the right place and at the right time. Wow! God is a master strategist. She could have refused to help Mordecai. She could have kept quiet about her lineage and saved herself from an awful fate. But she didn't. Her heart was open to God's call on her life. God tests our hearts to remind us that everything we are and everything we have is because of Him.

God Tested Esther's Faith

> *Then Esther sent this reply to Mordecai: 'Go, gather together all the Jews who are in Susa, and fast for me. Do not eat or drink for three days, night or day. My maids and I will do the same. And then, though it is against the law, I will go in to see the king. If I must die, I must die.*
>
> Esther 4:15-16

When God gives us a test of faith, it is meant to strengthen our relationship with Him. A faith test is a pathway that leads to our realization that we serve a trustworthy and faithful God. When our faith is tested, our relationship with our Creator is tested. I believe passing this God-given test requires us to prepare in a very particular way. We must choose Him daily allowing Him to supply us with the knowledge and strength we need to pass the test. He does this through our relationship with Him.

You see, God has already equipped us with the skills, abilities, and character we need to take the test and pass it. He has put us purposefully in the place and time of our testing. Our role in the test is to prepare for it, embrace it, and use the power He extends to us through our preparation to pass His test.

Esther's preparation included prayer and fasting for three days. She asked her people to join her and do the same. At the end of this time spent with God, she knew what she had to do. Dressing in her most beautiful royal garments, she went to visit the king—uninvited—risking his disfavor and her own death.

> *When he saw Queen Esther standing there in the inner court, he welcomed her and held out the gold scepter to her. So Esther approached and touched the end of the scepter.*
>
> Esther 5:2

She didn't enter the king's throne room unannounced without having spent time preparing for the test that was ahead. She waged her battle wearing the full armor of God. She knew the fight before her to save her people could not be won without supernatural intervention. By making her request known to God through prayer and fasting, Esther knew the outcome was up to God. When she entered the throne room prepared for any outcome. She was ready. Her faith was unshakeable. And the rest is history!

God Tested Esther's Obedience

If you keep quiet at a time like this, deliverance and relief for the Jews will arise from some other place, but you and your relatives will die. Who knows if perhaps you were made queen for just such a time as this?

Esther 4:14

I believe the obedience test is one that God gives to measure our trust in Him. If we trust, we obey. If we don't trust, we disobey. No matter which path we choose, we are communicating what we believe about God.

Esther was truly a model of obedience. She was taken from the only home she had ever known and given a life she never asked for much less imagined for herself. However, God had a plan for Esther's life—a purpose that only she could fulfill—and Esther had no idea. Her only choice was to trust God and be obedient.

While in the king's palace, Esther kept her identity as a Hebrew a secret, just as her uncle had told her to do. Esther obeyed. When Mordecai challenged Esther to save her people, Esther obeyed. What courage and obedience it must have taken to speak the words, "If I die, I die?" Esther was obedient to her family, her faith, and her God. Although she was afraid and risked her own death, Esther passed all three of her tests.

God wants us to welcome His testing. No matter the focus of the test, He wants you to have a heart open and focused on Him. He wants you to prepare for your test with an unshakeable faith that acknowledges God is in control. He wants us to be obedient and fulfill the call He places on our lives even when we can't see or understand it.

Our lives, just like Esther's, are about something altogether different—higher—and greater than you or I can imagine. The focus of our life is to love God with all our heart, soul, and mind. We must put no others before Him—even ourselves. And when we do this, even when things look bad and it seems like there is no way out, God will always make a way for us.

I've tried to put myself in Esther's place, would my faith have been strong enough to make this life-or-death choice? I hope so; but, more than that, I am determined to have that type of faith. I want to be bold and unshakeable in the face of any circumstance.

Don't fear the time of testing God will take you through. It doesn't have to be miserable. Think of it as refinement that will reveal anything in your life that needs changing. Taking the test—passing the test—is the only way to move forward—to step onto the new ground He has prepared for you—to experience joy and peace—to become who He wants you to be. God is for us, and He will accomplish so much more than we could on our own if we invite Him to guide and help us during His test.

> *Dear brothers and sisters, when troubles of any kind come your way, consider it an opportunity for great joy. For you know that when your faith is tested, your endurance has a chance to grow. So let it grow, for when your endurance is fully developed, you will be perfect and complete, needing nothing.*
>
> James 1:2

Take the test. beloved. Allow Him to shape your heart, mind, and spirit. And you will pass the test with flying colors!

Follow the Map

One of my favorite places in England is the maze at Hampton Court Palace. It's an intricate path with high walls, so determining the direction you are moving in, and the location of the exit can be difficult. But, once you find your way out of the maze, there is an ice cream truck and a royal souvenir shop waiting on you.

For me, mazes can be frustrating and even a bit scary—especially when I get lost! But the people at Hampton Court are genius. They give you a map before you enter. Because I had my very own GPS guide, I didn't have to worry. I could just enjoy the experience.

Winding my way through the high green hedges, I marveled at the beauty of the maze, the quiet places, the places dappled in light, the sweet scent of flowers, and the alternating cool and warmth of the air along the way. I never got lost. I never felt anxious. Why? Because I followed the map. When I found the exit, right where the map said it would be, I was so proud of myself. I was thankful for the journey through the maze, and I thoroughly enjoyed my ice cream cone!

Unfortunately, not all mazes are like the one at Hampton Court. I know one, that has very high walls, it's dark inside, it twists and turns, and awful monsters are lurking around each corner. And if you don't have a map, you are in trouble.

Have you seen the movie *The Maze Runner*? Great movie if you like dystopian worlds, quests for freedom, and teen angst. Thomas, the main character, arrives at this strange place and sees this massive stone maze. Everyone is talking about it. Naturally, he is curious about what's inside. He's drawn to the maze. He watches it, talks to the others about it, and dreams about it until he can't stand it any longer. He runs in. And we all know what happens after that, he is trapped there and must battle the monsters lurking inside. Ultimately, he loses a friend.

Imagine for just a moment that you are Thomas, the hero of the story. What would you do? Would you stay away from the maze? Would you run inside just like Thomas did? Would you even think to find a map to help you navigate the right path to take?

I believe the maze in this movie is a perfect example of the one we are all trying to navigate in terms of our sexuality. We hit puberty and experience sexual desire for the first time and then we are pushed into the maze. A maze created by our culture.

And this culture tells us we can have anything we want, anytime we want. It tells us we don't need to follow anyone's rules. It tells us sex is the end game in relationships and our own pleasure is most important.

Of course, we are curious, we want our freedom to do as we wish, and we want to be loved. We want so badly to fill the emptiness we feel inside with something tangible. And unfortunately, most of us are pushed into the maze with no map or at least not a complete one. So, we get lost. We get hurt. We wander aimlessly in the dark often getting caught by the monsters there.

If only we had a map. Guess what? God, the designer and director of it all gave us the map. And if we want to experience the fullness of what it means to be created by God as a sexual being, we've got to use it.

So how do you navigate your sexual desire? How do you understand your sexual longings? How do you withstand temptation? How do you practice purity in your relationships? What do you do with your sexual baggage, hurt, rejection, or trauma?

Today, there are a million different outlets that can lead us into finding the answers to our questions about sexuality: parents, peers, churches, media, porn, culture, and the list goes on. Unfortunately, the answers we find are rarely grounded in truth, morality, or scripture, but they should be.

All are a part of the world today. All are a part of our stories in some way. But before, we can answer any of these questions for ourselves, we must understand what sexuality is and value its important role in our life. The journey to understanding and valuing our sexuality needs to start at the very beginning, at the foundation. In its simplest, yet most complex form, sexuality is one thing and one thing only: spiritual!

I recognize that many of us weren't taught about the positive aspects of sexuality. We only know the negative. Or maybe we weren't taught anything about sexuality. And perhaps some of us never had the opportunity to see or experience our sexuality in a loving, life-giving way because we were placed in a horrible situation and were taken advantage of.

Seriously, so much of what we have learned, what we know, has come from popular media's distorted messages about sexuality. And because we lack an understanding of God's purpose for sexuality, it's no wonder that the rates of unhealthy relationships, porn addiction, and sexual assault are increasing. So how can we learn or even relearn everything we need to know about God's design of our sexuality?

Let me attempt to answer this question by asking one of my own: *What is sexuality?*

Our sexuality is a good gift given to us by God, our Creator.

> *Thank you for making me so wonderfully complex!*
> *Your workmanship is marvelous—how well I know*
> *it.*
>
> Psalms 139:14

His works are wonderful—that means us, the physical, the cognitive, the emotional, and the sexual us. The creation account in Genesis is clear, God is the gracious creator of everything in the universe, and anything He creates, including us and our existence as sexual beings is good. We have value.

Mo Isom writes in *Sex, Jesus and the Conversations the Church Forgot*, that we are sexual beings because sex is a deep and instructed desire in our hearts—placed there by God. He created our desire, our bodies, and their responses. He created it all.

Sex is much more than just a physical, mechanical act. I believe our sexuality engages the whole self: emotionally, relationally, socially, spiritually, and physically. Unfortunately, I think the conversations about sex education between many parents and their children have too often revolved around the mechanics of sex. What is really needed is a comprehensive discussion about the gift of our sexuality.

Maybe this was your experience in your home? Or, you had no instruction about sexuality at all. Whatever your experience, I believe it is important for you to know that your sexuality is the most intimate part of you. God's Word is clear if we take the time to read it, about what it means to be a godly woman who has also been gifted by God as a sexual being.

Our sexuality is designed and purposed by God.

This statement is true of young and old, female and male. He designed our bodies—bodies not to be ashamed of but bodies to be embraced and celebrated. He gave us the capacity for our sexual thoughts, feelings, and responses. I believe God made us sexual beings, not as an afterthought, but as a deliberate and intentional way to reveal His own character and nature.

It's like the swoosh on my Nike shoes. Nike is a brand with a specific logo that is recognized around the world. This swoosh tells you immediately that my shoe was made by Nike. When you see the swoosh, you think of speed, style, function, and price. The swoosh communicates value and purpose.

I've got a swoosh too. We all do. It's our bodies. Our bodies are the logo of our Designer. And this logo is supposed to be a symbol of Him. Even more than that, the logo, our bodies, are supposed to get you to think about the Designer. You are one of a kind, unique, and autographed. And as designers do, God numbers what He has made.

And the very hairs of your head are all numbered.

Matthew 10:30

Or what about...

And why worry about your clothing? Look at the lilies of the field and how they grow. They don't work or make their clothing, yet Solomon in all his glory was not dressed as beautifully as they are. And if God cares so wonderfully for wildflowers that are here today and thrown into the fire tomorrow, he will certainly care for you. Why do you have so little faith? "So don't worry about these things, saying, 'What will we eat? What will we drink? What will we wear?' These things dominate the thoughts of unbelievers, but your heavenly Father already knows all your needs. Seek the Kingdom of God above all else, and live righteously, and he will give you everything you need.

Matthew 6:28-33

And...

What is the price of five sparrows—two copper coins? Yet God does not forget a single one of them.

And the very hairs on your head are all numbered.
So don't be afraid; you are more valuable to God
than a whole flock of sparrows.

Luke 12:6-7

He dresses the lilies with beauty and splendor. He watches over every sparrow. How much more are you worth? How much more does He love you. More than you can imagine.

The design is clear, but, what about the purpose of our sexuality? Well, single or married, the first purpose of our sexuality is to teach us about God and His covenant love for us. John Piper, one of my favorite authors, says, "The ultimate purpose of our sexuality, the reason why we are sexual is to make God more deeply knowable."

The second purpose of our sexuality is reproduction! Sex generates life. Humanity can't continue without it. Without the joining of the sperm and egg to create life, we all cease to exist.

And the third purpose is passion and pleasure. Thank you, God! But here's the thing, sex is pleasurable because God designed it that way. He planned for sex to be terrific in a marriage where a husband and wife know each other intimately and exclusively. Sex is not designed to be a one-and-done, hook-up arrangement. It's intended between one man and one woman for life because on a level we will never completely understand; it knits one man and one woman together; they become "one flesh".

> *For this reason, a man will leave his father and mother and be united to his wife, and the two will become one flesh. This is a profound mystery.*
>
> Ephesians 5:31-33

Sex only within marriage is not a restrictive command, it's a solidifying one. It's the bedrock of the marital relationship. Honestly, it is God-designed "intimacy superglue." And even more than that, the solid bond of the one-flesh covenant within marriage is a real-time symbol of Christ's covenant with His bride—us—the church. Our sexual design is good, and its purpose is good. But they can both be distorted and even become harmful to us and others.

Pornography use and/or addiction are good examples. It is estimated that everyone living in the USA today has been or will be exposed to porn before they are an adult. According to the American Psychological Association, the average age for first exposure for boys and girls is between 11-13. Porn is literally everywhere, and anyone can access it, for free. Culture says porn is harmless; it's natural; it's good for you; it's a relationship booster.

But psychological and medical research shows something altogether different. In fact, scientists, like Dr. Valerie Voon, at the University of Cambridge, who study the brains of people who watch porn, are seeing some disturbing changes. MRI scans show that certain areas in the brains of people who watch porn are smaller than in the brains of people who don't watch porn.

The areas of the brain that are smaller are the ones responsible for empathy, compassion, and love. Porn shrinks the brain making the person consuming it more selfish, less compassionate, and less able to give and experience love and healthy relationships. That's science, y'all, not scripture!

Our sexuality is connected to God and should never be separated from Him

Before you get uncomfortable—or awkward—or think that God didn't have much to say about sexuality, think about this. Some of God's first words spoken over humanity were about our inherent value as His creation and about this act He called sex.

> *God made both male and female. And God wanted*
> *good to come to them, He blessed them saying, 'Give*
> *birth to many. Grow in number.'*
> Genesis 1:27-28

The Bible is very open and honest about sex from Genesis to Revelation. In fact, if you think about it, God is the first sex educator. The Bible begins with the covenant relationship of husband and wife, a marriage, and ends with a covenant relationship, Christ, the bridegroom returning for His bride. In fact, a whole book, the Song of Songs, celebrates the sensuality of erotic love. But there is a serious lack of conversation about sexuality and scripture, especially in the church. That's why it's a tough sell for us to latch on to this idea of connection because, for many of us, our views and thoughts about sex are in no way linked to our views and thoughts about God. For many of us, sex and God are polar opposites.

> *Don't let anyone capture you with empty philosophies and high-sounding nonsense that come from human thinking and from the spiritual powers of this world, rather than from Christ.*
>
> Colossians 2:8

In a 2014 article published in *The Christian Post*, a term was coined that fully represents this phenomenon, especially among Christian singles: sexual atheism. It is the disconnection of our Christian values and principles from our daily thoughts and actions regarding our sexuality. Sure, we believe in God and would call ourselves Christ-followers. We ask God to guide us, teach us, challenge us, rescue us, and bless us in every facet and circumstance of our life, except one— our sexuality. Consider this quote from the *Christian Post* article, "A person who at once believes in a wise, sovereign, and loving God who created them and all things, can also believe, at the same time, that God should not, cannot, or will not inform their life as a sexual being."

As Christians, we cannot afford to live the life of a sexual atheist. It will only lead to a painful dissonance in our lives. Our bodies, our souls, and our lives are not our own. They all belong to God. And how we use our bodies reveals what we believe about our Creator. We must pursue an "all-in" approach to the Word of God, the gospel of Christ. We were bought at a great price, and we need to start acting like it.

> *God bought you with a high price. So, you must honor God with your body.*
>
> I Corinthians 6:20

Many of you might think the only thing the Bible says about sex is "don't do it" and "sex is sinful." Maybe you think the Bible says nothing about sexuality and the challenges we all face today. Here's the thing: God's Word is full of sexual descriptions, guidelines, celebrations and so much more. And, if you are only looking for the word sex or sexuality in scripture then you are missing the bulk of what God says about it.

For example: Does scripture talk about dating?

When I ask my university students this question in our Marriage and Family class, most of my students say, "No, dating isn't in scripture at all!" Well, I disagree. If you are looking for the specific word "dating," you're right, it's not in the Bible. But the ways in which we should pursue and manage a dating relationship are in the Bible.

Here's an idea from the book, *Sex & the Supremacy of Christ*, that I borrowed from Dr. John Piper. Instead of looking for the word "dating" in scripture, search for the term "all things," instead. Why? Because a dating relationship, any kind of relationship for that matter, is a subset of "all things."

1 Corinthians 10:31, *Whatever you do, do **all** to the glory of God.*

The question to ask yourself then is: "How can my dating relationship bring glory to God?"

Sexuality is also a subset of "all things."

Colossians 1:16, *by Him **all things** were created.* Including Sex.

Ephesians 1:22, *God has put **all things** under the authority of Christ and has made him head over **all things** for the benefit of the church.* Including Sex.

1 Corinthians 10:31, *Whatever you do, do **all** to the glory of God.* Including Sex.

Our sexuality does bring glory to God, our Creator! And the list goes on. God and sexuality are irrevocably linked. They should never be separated. God is intentional. I have no doubt. You are His workmanship—His project—His creation—your sexuality included.

> *You made all the delicate, inner parts of my body and knit me together in my mother's womb. Thank you for making me so wonderfully complex! Your workmanship is marvelous—how well I know it. You watched me as I was being formed in utter seclusion, as I was woven together in the dark of the womb. You saw me before I was born. Every day of my life was recorded in your book. Every moment was laid out before a single day had passed.*
>
> Psalms 139:13-16

This brings me to my last point.

Our sexuality comes with real responsibility.

> *Imitate God, therefore, in everything you do, because you are his dear children. Live a life filled with love, following the example of Christ. He loved us and offered himself as a sacrifice for us, a pleasing aroma to God. Let there be no sexual immoral-*

ity, impurity, or greed among you. Such sins have no place among God's people.

Ephesians 5:1-3

How do we responsibly navigate our sexual desire, temptations, relationships, trauma, and the baggage we carry around? Let's revisit the maze.

Running culture's maze of sexuality can be done successfully if you use the map. God has given us the map we need to navigate the world's maze of sexuality: His Word. Scripture is the light that orders our steps and shows us the dead ends and crooked places, the wide paths, and safe spaces. If you try to run the maze without the map, you will be hopelessly lost, lonely, scared, frustrated, confused, or angry.

Because we have allowed the world around us to define our sexuality instead of defining it with the word of God, we have a distorted understanding of this good gift from our Father. I believe that the enemy of our souls has taken one of God's greatest gifts and is working diligently in this world to twist it and destroy it. And our distorted understanding and twisted version of sexuality offered have made it difficult for us to navigate the maze responsibly.

Let me stop right here and address an issue many women are struggling with today— virginity. A virgin is defined as someone who has never had sexual intercourse. We often use this standard to determine a woman's worth rather than evaluating the whole person. Unfortunately, using this standard as the bar for our sexual behavior is inadequate, confusing, and often damaging. In today's culture, virginity is a choice.

But what about the women who never had the opportunity to make the choice for virginity? What about the women who were molested or sexually abused in childhood? What about the women who have experienced a sexual assault? Are they less than whole, simply, because they are no longer virgins? No! Absolutely not!

What about women who made a mistake and were sexually active in the past? If they have sought forgiveness and restoration, are they not washed clean by the blood of the Lamb? And finally, is the issue really virginity, or is it purity?

> *But I say, anyone who even looks at another person with lust has already committed adultery with them in their heart.*
>
> Matthew 5:28

Christ is clear. Before we ever act, it is a matter of the heart. Christ focuses on our thoughts, feelings, and most of all our motivations because these precede our actions. Purity is a state of the mind and heart. Purity is freedom of immorality. Sinful action comes after we first have sinful thoughts or motivations. While virginity is an evaluation of the physical body, purity is an evaluation of the heart.

> *Create in me a clean heart, O God. Renew a loyal*
> *spirit within me.*
>
> Psalms 51:10

Seek purity in all things. Thought. Feeling. Action. Shift your focus. Purity is a choice—a decision you can make at any moment in your life. Purity is a commitment you can make regardless of your choices or experiences in your past. Living a life of purity brings freedom, not bondage. God's map for our sexuality is meant to protect, not to punish. Pursue purity.

As John Piper notes in *Sex & the Supremacy of Christ,* our sexuality is a pointer to God not a substitute for Him. Piper goes on to make two significant points. Our sexuality is designed by God as a way to know God in Christ more fully. And knowing God in Christ more fully is designed as a way of guarding and guiding our sexuality. He suggests that misuses of our sexuality distort the true knowledge of Christ and that these misuses derive from not having the true knowledge of Christ. Wow!

Never had the significance of the map and the maze been clearer to me than during my time as a high school counselor. I interacted with students daily who struggled with or were challenged by their development as sexual beings. One young woman I will never forget. She was fifteen, a great student, bright, vivacious, and couldn't wait to be a nurse. She was my aide in the counseling office during 4th period. So, I got to spend a lot of time with her.

She was dating a young man who was a senior at the time. Her family didn't approve of the relationship. I will never forget coming into my office one morning before school and she was there waiting on me. Her eyes were red and swollen from crying. She told me she was pregnant. I assured her that I would help in any way I could. I encouraged her to tell her parents. I told her she could still be a nurse. I told her this baby was a gift even though she might not see it that way now. We talked every week. Over the course of her nine-month journey to becoming a mother, she was heartbroken multiple times.

The young man who was the father of her child dropped out of school and left her. Her parents, who by the way had never talked with her about sex, kicked her out of the house. She went to live in a small room at her grandmother's house where she was reminded daily that she was a "bad girl." She had no job, was struggling in school, no family support, and not even a driver's license when she went into labor on a rainy Saturday morning in April.

I received a call from the hospital. Would I come? There was no one else with her and she wanted me. I held her hand that day as she labored to bring a beautiful baby boy into this world. I cried with her, coached her, and celebrated with her at the birth of her child. That day, one thing became crystal clear to me. Young people, just like this beautiful girl whose hand I was holding, needed guidance, training, education, support, encouragement, someone to stand in the gap for them, someone who would not only teach them about the sacredness and purpose of their sexuality but who would also teach their parents how to have these incredibly significant conversations with them. This experience forever changed my life. It's why I want to offer you these truths.

Your sexuality is a gift. God designed you as a sexual being for a good purpose. You are not alone in your desires, your struggles, your temptations, or your hurt. And you are not lost. God, your Creator, has given you the map of culture's maze. And He has freely offered His unfailing love, grace, forgiveness, and mercy to you along the way. Now, you get to decide if you're going to ask God to be your traveling companion in the maze and whether you will use His map.

Run the maze, beloved, just don't forget to follow the map.

Write Your Love Song

If you are browsing through new releases on Spotify, it won't be long before you run across a song about love. It seems like every other song released, from pop to country, is written about the total mind, body, and soul experience of love. If we could calculate the number of songs written about love since music was created, I'm confident its amount would be astronomical. I think it's safe to say we are a people in love with love and songs about love.

According to The Beatles, from their *Magical Mystery Tour* album, *"All you need is love...love is all you need."* Or how about "Love Hurts" by the 70's rock band, Nazareth? They sing *"Love hurts. Love scars. Love wounds and marks."* And then there's the country duo, Dan & Shay, crooning about love in their hit "From the Ground Up." *"And we'll build this love from the ground up. Now, 'til forever it's all of me, all of you. Just take my hand. And I'll be the man your dad hoped that I'd be."*

In "Thinking Out Loud," Ed Sheeran serenades us with lyrics about long-lasting love, *"When my hair's all but gone and my memory fades. And the crowds don't remember my name. When my hands don't play the strings the same way, I know you will still love me the same."* In her song "Love Story," Taylor Swift sings, *"Marry me, Juliet, you'll never have to be alone. I love you and that's all I really know. I talked to your dad, go pick out a white dress. It's a love story, baby just say yes!"*

And last but certainly not least, I can't leave out one of my favorite Dolly Parton songs, from her album *Love Like a Butterfly*, *"Love is like a butterfly, as soft and gentle as a sigh. The multicolored moods of love are like its satin wings. Love makes your heart feel strange inside. It flutters like soft wings in flight. Love is like a butterfly, a rare and gentle thing."* A butterfly, really?

Which song is true? Is it the one that's all about the romance you feel? Or the one that makes love the villain of everything that's gone wrong? Or the one that makes love sound easy and if it isn't then it wasn't right in the first place? What do you believe? If you could write your own love song, what would you say about love?

> *This is the first and greatest commandment. A second is equally important: 'Love your neighbor as yourself.*
>
> Matthew 22: 38-39

There is no value or human expression of greater importance than love. To the God who created us, love is huge. It is important. It is essential. Love is everything. God is love. And His love is eternal. Love God, first, love people as we love ourselves, second. If these things are true, and they most certainly are, then we must make loving well a priority in our lives.

In the Marriage and Family class I teach, we discuss the concept of love: emotion, thought, action, and experience. I ask my students, "What is love? What does it look like? Is 'I love my husband' the same as 'I love chocolate?'" I sure hope not! How can one word fully represent all the many complexities and subtle nuances of the emotions, thoughts, and actions that communicate love?

Sadly, because we only have one word for love in the English language, our culture has watered down and distorted the meaning of it to such a degree that sometimes it's hard to see its beauty, simplicity, and especially its depth. I would even go so far as to say that we, as a society, have become desensitized to the word love and the significant place it holds in our relationships. Our overuse of the word love to describe things both trivial and important has cheapened and confused its meaning.

Throughout scripture, in fact, in any translation written in English, the word "love" is singularly used to describe all its many facets. How can one word, and one word only, ever do it justice? So, to help my students understand the full breadth of the meaning and experience of love, I introduce them to three Hebrew words as defined in this ancient and foundational language of scripture. These words are *Ahava, Raya,* and *Dod.*

The first word, *ahava,* represents the devotion and commitment that is characteristic of love. The root word, *hav,* literally means "to give." The use of the word *ahava* to describe love shows us that the strength of a love relationship is found in giving. I believe *ahava* is the act of loving in its purest form. Think of it this way: *Ahava* is the embodiment of all five love languages wrapped into one. The acting out of love is affirmation, service, gifts, physical touch, and quality time, giving all, to the person we love.

Ahava honors your loved one. *Ahava* gives your love focus and purpose. *Ahava* isn't just a pretty word—it's an action. If you want to know the depth of someone's love for you, don't listen to their words, watch their feet. Words are easy, actions require effort. This word, *ahava,* is not founded in emotion but in the will. *Ahava* is the anchor in a relationship. *Ahava* says, "I choose you, today, tomorrow and forever."

> *Place me like a seal over your heart, like a seal on*
> *your arm; for love (ahava) is as strong as death, its*

jealousy unyielding as the grave. It burns like blazing fire, like a mighty flame. Many waters cannot quench love (ahava); rivers cannot sweep it away. If one were to give all the wealth of one's house for love (ahava), it would be utterly scorned.

Song of Solomon 8:6-7

Ahava is also used in scripture to describe the way in which we should love God. It's a ferocious love!

*Love (**ahava**) the LORD your God with all your heart and with all your soul and with all your strength.*

Deuteronomy 6:5

The second word, *raya*, describes the love we find in friendship and companionship. It could literally be translated as "soulmate". *Raya* is the love that is expressed and experienced in intimate conversation, the sharing of thoughts, dreams, and beliefs with another. *Raya* is the love between best friends.

Raya is love that never fades, even with age and circumstance. *Raya* says, "I love you—the you on the inside." *Raya* doesn't focus on the exterior, the physical appearance. It loves the deepest, most vulnerable places, inside you. It honors you and everything that has made you who you are, good and bad. *Raya* doesn't turn away from you. *Raya* looks you straight in the eye, right into the heart of you, and loves you just the same.

King Solomon says it best,

> *You are altogether beautiful, my love (**raya**); there is no flaw in you.*
>
> Song of Songs 4:7

The third word, *dod*, is a powerful word that means "to fondle." Seriously, all blushing and giggles aside, *dod* is defined as passion and pursuit. It is the attraction, sexual love, connection, and romantic feelings that are a part of a physical love relationship found within the covenant of marriage. *Dod* says, "I am attracted to you. I want to be your lover." The word *dod* is used, over and over again, in the Song of Songs to illustrate the physical love and wanting that is experienced by a husband and wife.

King Solomon's wife says,

> *May he kiss me with the kisses of his mouth, for his love (**dod**) is better than wine.*
>
> Song of Songs 1:2

Ahava, Raya and *Dod*. When these three types of love are united in one covenant relationship, something greater is created. A love that is strong, unquenchable, and lasting. One love without the presence of the other three is less vibrant and fulfilling. But the true meaning of these three words, their real purpose, is to show us how God loves us and the ways in which we should love God.

My beloved is mine and I am His.

Song of Songs 2:16

God loves you with a commitment, *ahava*, that will never be broken. He is unselfish in His care and provision for you. He loves you ferociously.

God loves you intimately—the you that no one else can see. He wants to be your best friend. He desires intimacy, *raya*, with you.

God loves you with an epic passion. You are the object of his affection and His pursuit. He wants to be your *dod*, your beloved.

I was unable to move forward, closer, to my soul-longings, until I learned this valuable lesson. A relationship with my beloved is what my soul was longing for. Only when I learned to love and be loved in return in my relationship with God did I come to understand the beauty, purpose, and power of love.

Recognizing real love, God's plan for love, apart from the distorted, watered-down, and dysfunctional love, that our culture surrounds us with, is probably the most important lesson I learned on my journey. I believe it will be the same for you. Embrace God's multi-faceted love for you. Come to know Him intimately. Commit yourself to Him completely. Pursue a relationship with Him passionately. Make loving God a priority. When you do, your perspective will shift. No matter the heartbreak you may have experienced in your life, a love relationship with Him will mend your heart. It will fill the empty and perhaps damaged places in your soul. God is love, so the more you know Him, the more you will know what love is.

During this time in my journey, there was a song that not only became dear to me because it spoke so deeply to my soul, but it also became my guide to understanding God's love for me.

It's entitled *Reckless Love* and it was written by Cory Asbury. Here is an excerpt:

Before I spoke a word, You were singing over me
You have been so, so good to me
Before I took a breath, You breathed Your life in me
You have been so so kind to me

Oh, the overwhelming, never-ending,
reckless love of God
Oh, it chases me down,
fights 'til I'm found,
leaves the 99

And I couldn't earn it
I don't deserve it,
still You give yourself away

Oh, the overwhelming, never-ending,
reckless love of God

Don't settle for a love that is anything less than overflowing with *raya, ahava* and *dod*. Don't let your insecurities, lack of self-esteem, and your belief that you have no value or worth on your own, rule your choices. Let love, God's love for you, guide the decisions you make in your life. Let God's love lead you in your relationships with others. Invite God to be the co-writer of your love song.

To ensure that your love song, doesn't become a one-hit-wonder, but instead becomes a Grammy-award winner for "best song of all time," you cannot forget to also love the people around you, even those that are unloveable. God has called each of us to show His love to others, including those you cannot understand or those that may have hurt you. The divine example of God's Son, Jesus Christ, is His perfect love and forgiveness.

Did I just say forgiveness? Yeah, I did! In my own broken relationship, it was tough for me to say "I forgive you" but even more challenging was the effort it took to act on the forgiveness. Sometimes the hurt is so deep, that it's difficult to see beyond our pain and grief. But, if you hold on to the hurt refusing to let it go, it will come to define who you are.

True forgiveness requires you to make a conscious and deliberate decision. And often you will need to make that decision every day until it becomes second nature. Forgiveness takes time, patience, and perseverance. It will require you to release the anger, pain, and resentment you feel toward the person who betrayed, hurt, or violated you. Even if they don't deserve it. This act of forgiveness is for you, not for the other person. To love and be loved as God has planned for you, your heart must be full of Him and not hate. Forgiving another person takes courage.

Trying to find meaning in our suffering is critical. And finding this meaning does not in any way diminish or ignore the suffering you have experienced. Forgiveness doesn't mean staying in a relationship or even resuming one if significant changes have not been made—changes that may require the eradication of certain thoughts, actions, or emotions. Forgiveness doesn't mean forgetfulness or the acceptance of anything less than real change. Forgiveness doesn't mean that you forget the injustice, nor do you condone the behavior. You forgive because you are choosing to show mercy despite it all.

Psychologist, Robert Enright, a pioneer in the scientific study of forgiveness, says, "The forgiveness process, properly understood and used, can free those bound by anger and resentment. It does not require accepting injustice or remaining in an abusive situation. It opens the door to reconciliation, but it does not require trusting someone who has proven untrustworthy. Even if the offender remains unrepentant, you can forgive and restore a sense of peace and well-being to your life. The choice is yours."

Participating in the act of forgiveness is not only good for your heart, but also for your mind and your body too. Psychological research has shown that when we forgive others, we experience many psychological benefits. Forgiving instead of resenting will elevate your mood and your overall sense of well-being. Forgiving instead of hating will help to level your emotions so you can experience peace. Forgiving instead of seeking revenge will enhance your optimism and positivity about life and others.

Most of all, forgiving instead of holding a grudge will protect you, acting as a buffer, between you and negative emotions like anger, stress, anxiety, and depression. Forgiving another person is like medicine for healing deep wounds. Forgiveness is extending goodness, grace, and mercy to another person mirroring the forgiveness that Jesus Christ offers us through his sacrifice.

What if the person you need to forgive is yourself? Face it, we tend to be much harder on ourselves than we are on others. And I would dare say, we have all had moments in our life that we wish we could take back—maybe those moments are days, months, or years, even. We have said unkind words. We have lost our tempers. We have treated another person critically or harshly. We have betrayed someone or some principle. We have stood still when we should have moved, or the other way around. And soon, it all starts piling up, dragging us down a deep well of self-loathing. It's a struggle to love a person you hate, especially if that person is you. But, just as every good thing we have ever done doesn't totally define us, neither does every bad thing.

It's time to stop punishing yourself for whatever you did, said, thought, or felt. If you don't, you risk not being able to write your love song at all. Stop beating yourself up for something you did wrong. Do your best to make it right, be accountable, and move on. In the same way, you would soften your heart and show compassion to another person, you must do the same for yourself. You must offer yourself the same forgiveness you offer others.

We can see the greatest example of love and forgiveness in the life of God's Son, Jesus Christ. His life, all thirty-three years of it, His ministry, and His sacrifice, were all for us. Without Him, the plan of salvation would have failed. We would be lost forever and consigned to a life of sin and death.

On His last day on this earth, Christ experienced unfathomable hurt, rejection, abuse, and betrayal, even at the hands of those He loved.

Peter

The guards lit a fire in the middle of the courtyard and sat around it, and Peter joined them there. 5A servant girl noticed him in the firelight and began staring at him. Finally, she said, "This man was one of Jesus's followers! But Peter denied it. "Woman," he said, "I don't even know him!" After a while, someone else looked at him and said, "You must be one of them!" "No, man, I'm not!" Peter retorted. About an hour later someone else insisted, "This must be one of them, because he is a Galilean, too." But Peter said, "Man, I don't know what you are talking about." And immediately, while he was still speaking, the rooster crowed. At that moment the Lord turned and looked at Peter. Suddenly, the Lord's words flashed through Peter's mind: "Before the rooster crows tomorrow morning, you will deny three times that you even know me." And Peter left the courtyard, weeping bitterly.

Luke 22: 54-62

Judas

Then Satan entered into Judas Iscariot, who was one of the twelve disciples, and he went to the leading priests and captains of the Temple guard to discuss the best way to betray Jesus to them. They were delighted, and they promised to give him money. So he agreed and began looking for an opportunity to betray Jesus so they could arrest him when the crowds weren't around.

Luke 22:3-6

While He was still speaking, a crowd arrived, led by the man called Judas, one of the Twelve. He approached Jesus to kiss Him. But Jesus asked him, "Judas, are you betraying the Son of Man with a kiss?"

Luke 22: 47-48

The Crowd

Wanting to release Jesus, Pilate addressed them again, but they kept shouting, "Crucify Him! Crucify Him!"
A third time he said to them, "What evil has this man done? I have found in Him no offense worthy of death. So after I punish Him, I will release Him."

But they were insistent, demanding with loud voices for Jesus to be crucified. And their clamor prevailed. So Pilate sentenced that their demand be met. As they had requested, he released the one imprisoned for insurrection and murder, and handed Jesus over to their will.
And His suffering on the cross was indescribable. Carrying the cross by himself, he went to the place called Place of the Skull (Golgotha). There they nailed him to the cross.

John 19:17-18

And yet, He forgave them all.

Father, forgive them, for they don't know what they are doing.

Luke 23:34

All three of these examples of Christ offering forgiveness to those who had hurt him, demonstrate the power of forgiveness. God has given us the divine power to forgive. Forgiveness leads to healing—your healing. Forgiving the person who wronged you will push you forward on your journey to find what your soul longs for. Give it all to God and allow him to exchange your ashes for beauty.

Beloved, I can't wait to hear the love song that you and God will write together!

Become a Warrior Heroine

Once upon a time. The best stories begin this way. And if you are anything like me, you immediately want to know what happens next. I love a great story. One full of adventure with romance, challenge, and triumph. I especially love the happy ending that I know is coming if I just hang on until the end. I am a literary geek, and I am proud of it! And, yes, the book is always better than the film.

As a psychologist, I have spent my professional career studying the ins and outs of human behavior and I am immensely fascinated by the human experience. I daresay we all are, on some level. I think that's why stories can have a profound impact on our lives. Stories are the language of the heart. We identify with the vivid characters who live between the pages of a novel in deep and meaningful ways. We emotionally connect with them—their strengths and flaws, joy and sorrow, successes, and failures, and even their suffering. We learn more about ourselves by reading about them. We learn valuable lessons from their fictional experiences that we can apply to our own lives.

Some of the greatest characters in literature are women. From a small-town teenage detective to a medieval shieldmaiden, these literary heroines, transport us to other worlds, places, times, and experiences. The storyline for each heroine includes a challenging journey, exciting adventures, danger, some suffering, maybe a love relationship, a pivotal moment of self-realization, a villain that must be defeated, and a happy ending to enjoy. They inspire us. They teach us. Their experiences are our experiences. Their stories mirror our own. And these characters stay with us long after we finish reading the novels, they are featured in.

These literary heroines are certainly not perfect. In fact, most of them are a little quirky and even awkward at times. Like us, just women minding their own business trying to make the best life possible for themselves amid mistakes, triumphs, heartbreak, love, emotions, and the curveballs of adversity life likes to throw their way sometimes. To be honest, there are many days, I will come home, curl up on my couch with my favorite blanket, and read one of my favorite novels. Then I am quickly immersed in a fictional world where anything is possible, and every woman can be a heroine despite the odds. I think my time spent with these literary heroines has actually boosted my confidence more times than not. I have learned some valuable life lessons from these fictional women.

From Elizabeth Bennett, in *Pride and Prejudice*, I was challenged to never settle for less or change who I am to live up to society's expectations.

From Nancy Drew, in the *Nancy Drew* series, I learned to fearlessly pursue the truth and keep asking questions.

From Aibileen, in *The Help*, I discovered the importance of loving myself and helping others to do the same.

From Anne Shirley, in *Anne of Green Gables*, I was inspired to choose joy, no matter the circumstance. She also taught me that red hair and freckles were cool!

From Katniss Everdeen, in *Hunger Games*, I realized that I can be brave and fight a good fight, even when I am scared.

From Jane Eyre, in *Jane Eyre*, I understood that even if it is the most difficult thing to do, I can get back up and keep moving forward.

From Scarlett O'Hara, in *Gone with the Wind*, I recognized that with determination, I can rise from the ashes and be a survivor.

From Angel, in *Redeeming Love*, I accepted that I could break free of any circumstance and let go of my past because it doesn't define me.

And from Ella, in *Cinderella*, I embraced the best lesson of all—never lose hope.

They all faced insurmountable odds, embraced their destinies, and won the day. Each heroine, unique in her design, was equipped with special talents and abilities. Each one had to risk and fight for what she believed. Their stories are fantasies.

What about real accounts of warrior women in history? I believe the most powerful real-life examples of warrior heroines are found in scripture.

We can look throughout scripture and see countless real-life stories of women who were special. Not because they were the most beautiful, the smartest, the purest, or the wealthiest. Special because God designed them, equipped them, prepared them, and placed them in a specific place— a battleground—to fight and to facilitate his story—his plan—paving the way for His son, Jesus Christ. Their hearts—their choices—their obedience—their faith and trust made the difference in the outcome. They all faced incredible challenges, pain, loss, trauma, harassment, and even death but still, they remained bright lights in a dark world.

Here is just a glimpse of all the wonderful wisdom I gleaned from the study of these warrior heroines:

From Eve, the first woman, I know I should never underestimate the plans of the enemy.

From Sarai, the mother of nations, who struggled to trust God, I realize that God always keeps His promises.

From Hagar, a servant, a nobody, I learn that we are all seen by God and loved just the same.

From Deborah, Israel's only female judge, who lived her life always trusting in the word of God even when others doubted, I grasp the power of the testimony of faith!

From Jael, a wife and homemaker, who fulfilled an incredible prophecy in war through her bold and courageous spirit, I recognize the value of acting without hesitation on every opportunity God may place in front of me.

From Esther, the queen, I understand the significance of preparing for battle and the reward for risking big and leaving the outcome to God.

From Ruth, a widow in a foreign land, I see that God will provide my heart's desires.

From Mary, the mother of Jesus, I appreciate that I can trust God even in the face of the impossible and that He can use me even if I don't believe in myself.

From the Woman with the Issue of Blood, who let nothing stop her from touching Jesus Christ, I discover the power of relentless pursuit.

From the Woman at the Well, despite her many failed relationships and loss of reputation, I accept that I am loved for who I am, and the past doesn't matter when we make the choice to live for Christ.

From Mary Magdalene, a woman healed of demonic spirits, who became a disciple of Christ, I know without a doubt that God loves to use women to spread the gospel.

From Lois and Eunice, grandmother and mother to the apostle Timothy, I note the importance and ultimate reward of raising my children in a home filled with love, faith and the pursuit of a relationship with God.

From Mary and Martha, sisters and friends of Jesus Christ, I embrace that time spent with my Savior is more important than anything else I could ever do.

And the list goes on.

These women are the warrior heroines of the Bible. Women engaged in warfare of all kinds—physical, emotional, psychological, and spiritual. Women who beyond all obstacles still managed to overcome. Women who were troubled in life but persevered to the end. Overcoming and conquering require guts and these women had both.

Where did this courage come from? From God, Our Father. Each woman was dramatically different in personality, life experience, strengths, and weaknesses. Each one was unique. But all of them were warriors.

These remarkable women possessed a certain mentality—one that helped them overcome and conquer the challenges they were presented in their lives. They developed and were able to maintain this warrior mindset in the face of great obstacles by drawing strength, courage, and resolve, from their relationship with their Creator. The mindset of a warrior heroine is achieved as the result of the journey to finding what your soul longs for.

How does one become a warrior heroine?

- She dares to trust and with her focus on Him, she decides to change her life by getting out of her boat.
- She looks honestly at her reflection in the mirror and accepts the value and worth of the woman she sees there.
- She unpacks her suitcase full of shame, failure, and mistakes and forges ahead with a lighter load.
- She asks tough questions, even though the answers she finds might be tough to embrace.
- She lets down her hair and leaves her tower full of lies and her idols behind.
- She plays the waiting game and remains steadfast in her trust in God's timing and purpose
- She avoids relationship traps and pursues her relationship with God first.
- She looks fear in the face, takes her Father's hand, and moves forward confidently, refusing to be afraid of the dark.
- She allows God to shape her heart, mind, and spirit and she passes the tests she is given.
- She follows the map and asks God to join her on her journey through culture's maze of sexuality.

- She writes a love song with lyrics that sing of God's love and the power of forgiveness.

I believe you are a warrior heroine! You might not see her when you look in the mirror. But she is there—right below the surface. Set her free. How would you live differently if you believed this to be true? God has been calling to you all the days of your life. You've heard Him on the wind and in the waves, in laughter and in tears, and most especially in the stories that have captured your heart. He wrote a secret on your heart, sweet daughter. You are fearfully and wonderfully made for such a time as this. You can write your own story.

You can fight your battles with your warrior spirit. With focus and discipline, you can push forward in the face of challenges confident that you will overcome and be resilient. Why? Because you serve an all-powerful God, who will never let us fight alone.

> *For the Lord your God is going with you! He will fight for you against your enemies, and he will give you victory!*
>
> Deuteronomy 20:4

Don't ride in the passenger seat of life, just going through the motions. Don't sacrifice your role as a heroine to take on the role of a victim. To become the warrior heroine of your own story, you must remain focused on the blessings and challenges that greet you each day, and not the ones that may or may not come tomorrow, and certainly not the ones from the past.

Remember, I said this before we started, the journey to what your soul longs for won't be easy—nothing worth accomplishing or experiencing ever is. And shortcuts on the type of trip we are on won't help you arrive any sooner at your destination. True growth and learning require a long journey. But the journey can be simple. Allow God and the power you receive through your relationship with Him to make you strong, wise, and victorious.

Beloved, you can write and re-write the script for the role you want to take. Be the warrior heroine in the story of your life!

Step onto the Shore

When I finally stepped onto the shore at the end of my journey, the joy I felt was indescribable. I was exhausted yet felt more alive than ever. I had left the anxious, damaged, fearful woman of my past behind. No longer diminished, I was secure in His love for me and as a result, I was emboldened to be me. I had made it. I felt lighter—stronger—fuller—I felt like a whole person.

I smiled and wiggled my toes in the warm sand. I lifted my face to the bright sun and soft breeze. I listened to the sound of the waves rolling onto the shore bringing with them a profound sense of peace and quietness to my soul. The woman standing on the shore was the woman God had created me to be. I know now that I am good enough. I am an overcomer. I am loved. I am valued. I am safe. I am His daughter. My heart, soul, and mind are now exclusively fixed on Him. He is my source. He is my everything. I am blessed and highly favored because He loves me.

That's when I realized that my journey wasn't about finding what my soul longed for—to be loved. The real purpose of the journey and its reward was becoming what my soul longed for—His beloved. I am a woman fully surrendered to God, dwelling in His presence, and living a life unashamedly for Him. The journey to the place I am now wasn't easy, but it was simple. Why? Because all I had to do was to ask my Lord and Savior to walk beside me. And He did, just like He did for Peter in the middle of a storm in the early morning hours on the Sea of Galilee.

It wasn't too long after my journey that God birthed a dream in my spirit. I wanted the young women who sit in my classroom, day after day, at my university to understand how valuable and worthy they were — something I didn't understand or recognize when I was a young woman. I wanted God's beloved daughters to know their identity was not found in what they do or don't do, what they look like or don't look like, or how they feel or don't feel. They needed to know the truth— their identity is found in our beloved, God, our Father.

The desire for a community in reckless pursuit of God led to the creation of Beloved, a women's Bible study community. We meet in the basement of my house once a week and dig deep into the word of God.

My prayer on the very first night we met together was: "God, please order the steps of the women who need to hear Your Word and Your Voice, to find their way to my home." God has honored my prayer every week since. Our Beloved community has grown exponentially by God's grace and provision.

My vision for Beloved is the same one I have for all women including myself. Simply, I want us to truly discover this truth of who we are. To know it—accept it—embrace it—never doubt it. I long for us to let our Creator's love, God, our Beloved, fill us in a way that we see ourselves as forever changed. My desire is for every woman, young, old, and everything in-between, to see herself as God sees her.

My wish is that a spark will be ignited in you that enlarges into a fire that will burn for a lifetime. The Creator of the universe, the God of angel-armies, the Lover of your soul is ordering your steps. He is giving you grace for each new day. He is restoring and redeeming your heart, mind, and soul. He is calling your name, beloved. Pursue Him above all else. He will go before you, walk alongside you and give you that little extra push you might need from behind when you need it most. His promises are true! He did it for me and I am confident He will do the same for you.

Will you get out of your boat and commit to the journey before you?

It won't be easy, but it will be simple. I challenge you to take the first step of many, the one that will ultimately lead you to all that your soul longs for. Leave your boat behind. Look for Him in the storm. He is there waiting for you. Take His Hand. Follow Him to the shore into your future bright with love, peace, joy, and purpose. Take to heart, the words of C.S. Lewis, "You can't go back and change the beginning, but you can start where you are and change the ending."

Come join me on the shore, beloved. The view is great!

References & Resources

Chambers, Oswald (1989). *The Place of Help*. Discovery House Publishing.

Clark, Alicia H. (2018). *Hack Your Anxiety: How to Make Anxiety Work for You in Life, Love, and All That You Do*. Sourcebooks.

Enright, Robert (2019). *Forgiveness is a Choice: A Step-by-Step Process for Resolving Anger and Restoring Hope*. American Psychological Association Life Tools.

Gottman, John. (2015). *Seven Principles for Making Marriage Work: A Practical Guide from the Country's Foremost Relationship Expert*. Harmony House.

Groeschel, Craig (2010). *The Christian Atheist: Believing in God but Living as if He Doesn't Exist*. Zondervan.

Isom, Mo (2018). *Sex, Jesus and the Conversations the Church Forgot*. Baker Books.

Keller, Timothy (2011). *Counterfeit Gods: The Empty Promises of Money, Sex, and Power, and the Only Hope that Matters.* Penguin Books

Kelly, Y., Zilanawala A., Booker C., & Sacker A. (2018). Social media use and adolescent mental health: findings from the *UK Millennium Cohort Study.* DOI:https://doi.org/10.1016/j.eclinm.2018.12.005

Luck, K. (2014, October). "Sexual Atheism: Christian Dating Data Reveals a Deeper Spiritual Malaise". *The Christian Post.* https://www.christianpost.com/news/sexual-atheism-christian-dating-data-reveals-a-deeper-spiritual-malaise.html

McCain, Paul. (Ed.), *Martin Luther's Large Catechism* (2010). Concordia Publishing.

Piper, John (2012). *Future Grace: The Purifying Power of the Promises of God.* Multnomah.

Piper, John & Taylor, Justin. (Eds.) (2005), *Sex and Supremacy of Christ.* Crossway.

Voon, V., Mole, T., Banca, P., Porter, L., Morris, L., Mitchell, S., Lapa, T., Karr, J., Harrison, N., Potenza, M., & Irvine, M. (2014). Neural Correlates of Sexual Cue Reactivity in Individuals with and without compulsive sexual behaviors. https://doi.org/10.1371/journal.pone.0102419

www.commonsensemedia.org
www.fherehab.com

www.fightthenewdrug.com

www.free.messianicbible.com

www.gamedeveloper.com

www.hopkinsmedicine.org

www.ipsos.com

www.kff.org

www.nationaleatingdisorders.org

www.news.illinoisstate.edu

www.nih.gov

www.online.king.edu

www.nedc.com.au

www.scholarsrepository.llu.edu

www.statista.com